The Beauty of
IRELAND

The Beauty of
IRELAND
by
Leslie Gardiner

Malin Head

Lough Foyle
• Portrush
• Coleraine
• Limavady
Londonderry
LONDONDERRY
R Foyle
• Ballymena
• Larne
DONEGAL **Lifford**
U L S T E R
Sperrin Mts
NORTHERN IRELAND
ANTRIM
Belfast Lough
• Donegal
• Omagh
TYRONE
Belfast
• Bangor
Donegal Bay
Ballyshannon
Lower L Erne
DOWN
Armagh
Downpatrick
• Enniskillen
FERMANAGH
ARMAGH
• Newry
• Newcastle
Sligo •
SLIGO
Upper L Erne
Monaghan
MONAGHAN
Iron Mts
Mourne Mts
• Ballina
Lough Conn
LEITRIM
Cavan
Carlingford L
Dundalk
Achill Island
• Boyle
Carrick-on-Shannon
CAVAN
LOUTH
Clew Bay
• **Castlebar**
C O N N A U G H T
• Castlerea
• **Longford**
• Kells
• Drogheda
• Westport
MAYO
ROSCOMMON
Roscommon
LONGFORD
• Navan
MEATH
Lough Mask
Mullingar
R Boyne
• Trim
Lough Corrib
GALWAY
Lough Ree
Athlone
WESTMEATH
DUBLIN
Royal Canal
Dublin
• **Galway**
Ballinasloe
Grand Canal
KILDARE
• Dun Laoghaire
Galway Bay
Tullamore
OFFALY
Kildare
R Liffey
• Naas
WICKLOW
Aran Islands
R Shannon
Slieve Bloom Mts
L E I N S T E R
• Glendalough
Wicklow
• Liscannor
Lough Derg
Portlaoise
LAOIS
Wicklow Mts
R Avonmore
CLARE
REPUBLIC OF IRELAND
• Carlow
• Arklow
• Ennis
R Barrow
R Slaney
• **Limerick**
• **Kilkenny**
CARLOW
• Listowel
LIMERICK
TIPPERARY
KILKENNY
R Nore
WEXFORD
Mouth of the Shannon
• Cashel
• **Tralee**
• Tipperary
Clonmel
Carrick on Suir
Wexford
KERRY
M U N S T E R
R Suir
• Dingle
• Fermoy
Waterford
Dingle Bay
• Killarney
WATERFORD
• Tramore
Valentia Island
Macgillycuddy's Reeks
Dungarvan
Hook Head
CORK
Youghal
• Ardmore
• **Cork**
Mizen Head
• Cobh
Bantry Bay
• Bantry
• Kinsale

A T L A N T I C   O C E A N

I R I S H   S E A

This edition produced in 1984
exclusively for Dunnes Stores by
Treasure Press
59 Grosvenor Street
London W1

© 1981 Octopus Books Ltd

ISBN 1 85051 034 2

Printed in Hong Kong

Contents

The publishers wish to thank Bord Fáilte (Irish Tourist Board) and the Northern Ireland Tourist Board for their help in providing the majority of the photographs in this book.

Endpapers: O'Donoghue's public house in Dublin.
Half-title: A farmer pauses outside his picturesque croft.
Title: A fishing boat moored at Burtonport, Donegal.

Foreword

Perched on a neck of land between Loughs Conn and Cullin, Pontoon offers splendid trout and salmon fishing. The slightly military flavour of the name recalls Cromwellian days, when a defensive system was organized along 160 km (100 miles) of loughs and rivers. Now the Pontoon district is peaceful and intensely colourful, part of rural Mayo, which claims to be 'the last great tranquillizer'.

Thousands of foreign visitors come to Ireland every year. There are many reasons why they are drawn to this island not the least of which is that their roots are here: the descendants of Irish emigrants, so many of whom live in America, Australia and in the rest of the British Isles, still feel the pull of this extraordinary land as the country to which they truly belong. Others come simply for a relaxing holiday, to explore Dublin's faded splendour, the tranquil landscape of brown turf and fertile rolling pastureland, or the bleak and desolate mountains, loughs and magnificent shoreline.

However you explore Ireland, either by going there or through this book, you will find yourself in a land steeped in magic, myth, folklore and history which seem inextricably intertwined: the heroic tales and legends with which every Irish child grows up seem to have shaped the country's character as much as the Act of Union or the disastrous potato famines which led to the rapid depopulation of the country in the late 1840s. This is the mythical *Tir-nan-Og*, the land of lost content, where giants like Finn MacCool are said to have walked, and where leprechauns are said to haunt the hedgerows.

The roadside shrines and holy places one passes on the quiet winding roads (where one can travel for miles without seeing another vehicle) remind the visitor that this is also an island of saints. St Patrick and St Kevin established the Church in Ireland, while Irish travelling monks took Christianity all over Europe; they are still venerated and celebrated in local ceremonies throughout the country.

The Romans christened the island Winter (*Hibernia*) and never came.

In the year 1700 the Irish suffered an invasion of a different sort, inspired by the re-awakening of interest in Roman art and architecture that is associated with the name of Andrea Palladio. The evidence remains to be seen in town and country houses. By 1800 a taste for the Gothic had begun to rival this classical tradition. The castle, abandoned after the Battle of the Boyne in 1690, was once more in fashion. Bogus battlements and arrow-slits enliven the skyline and it appeals to the ancestor-worshipper to see his coat of arms emblazoned on some mock port-cullis.

Ireland also has rich literary associations: this is the native land of Swift, Shaw, Wilde, Yeats, Synge and Joyce, names now famous throughout the world. And one only has to meet the Irish to realize how it is that their fellow-countrymen have given us such riches. A peculiarly Irish attitude to life shows itself in a relaxed, easy-going outlook which so delights other English speakers who never quite achieve the poetic fluency of the native Irish. It is the people, essentially who give this country its richness: they have imbued the landscape with the romance and mythology which fascinates all who land on the shores of the 'Emerald Isle'.

Desmond Guinness

The Honourable Desmond Guinness
Founder of the Irish Georgian Society

Shimmering waters, tongues of rocks, a simple cabin, a rudimentary boat-landing: such are the components of west-of-Ireland lakescapes. This is Lough Aunfree, in the delightful region of Connemara, County Galway.

Introduction

On a first visit, Ireland is just as you would imagine it to be: cheerful, slow-paced, with a population of individualists. It is a country where words speak louder than actions, for the Irish are voluble and persuasive talkers.

In a restful, casual way quite a lot is happening. In the city there are horse trials, open-air pop concerts, Gaelic football finals, crowds massing for a hurling match or at a theatre where Shaw, Wilde, Yeats or Synge are bound to be playing. In the countryside you cannot escape eccentric festivals and ceremonies, some pious and some pagan.

The romance and mythology of the Emerald Isle are inescapable. The Bells of Shandon can be plainly heard. The Blarney Stone is a genuine stone. At road junctions we shall sooner or later see signposts for Donnybrook, Shillelagh, Innisfree, Ballyjamesduff (*Come back, Paddy Reilly*) and other places immortalized in song and legend. The Mountains of Mourne are visible, and so are Galway Bay, the Rock of Cashel, the Killarney lakes, the Giant's Causeway and the sweet Vale of Avoca. An Irish guide will indicate with perfect confidence the sunken city in Lough Neagh, the hilltop from which Saint Patrick banished all the snakes, the narrow glen where the blackbird laid her eggs in Saint Kevin's hand, and the three authentic birthplaces of the first Duke of Wellington. The Colleen Bawn has become an operatic heroine and a Rose of Tralee springs forth at a beauty contest every year.

The successions of magnificent seascapes on the 'Atlantic Drives', 'Brandy-and-Soda Roads' and other invigorating routes round Ireland, prompt many to tour the country with an automobile, a bicycle or a self-drive horse-drawn

caravan. South from Dublin the coastal routes touch at somnolent half-tide harbours on the way to Wexford's long waterfront. Round the corner, Waterford's thronged quays and foreign-registered shipping hint that Ireland, after all, is in touch with a world of commerce and industry.

American and Continental visitors like to head for the sub-tropical south-western peninsulas of the 'Kingdom' of Kerry. The north-eastern corner still holds attractions for English and Scottish holidaymakers. Here are the venerable North of Ireland resorts of the Ards peninsula ('the comely Ards, the pleasant Ards, the land of little hills'). Under dark Mourne there lies a soft country sprinkled with clean farmsteads and well-tamed sands stretching all the way to Howth and Malahide, the seaside suburbs of Dublin. At the end of a complete circuit of Ireland, the visitor feels he has seen everything. But that was only the coast.

Inland voyages, by road or leafy canal, are journeys through an old-time rustic tranquillity. Beech trees touch branches across the road, walls and hedges are festooned with fuchsia and rose, kingfishers dart from canal banks, wrought-iron shrines mark the passage of the miles and, under a creeper-covered bridge, a priest sits angling for Friday's lunch. On Ireland's hinterland of byways the motorist discovers the lost joys of motoring, travelling for miles without seeing any traffic but a donkey-cart or postman's bicycle.

The meandering railway train rarely encounters a hill or a tunnel, but passengers are hardly ever out of sight of the coastal ring of mountains – folded granite of Wicklow, quartz of Connemara, limestone of Clare and old red sandstone of Kerry. That sheltering saucer-ring of hills, draining towards the centre, gives Ireland its emerald turf and prolific botany of the hedgerows.

Studied on the map, Ireland occupies an intriguing situation. It evades the embrace of Scottish, Welsh and English promontories and dips a foot in the profound depths of the Atlantic. It is the first land we see when travelling from New World to Old, the last when heading from Old to New. It is natural to associate Ireland with ideas of a Golden West, an Isle of Saints, the last vestiges of prehistoric Europe and the mythical country of perpetual youth which the Irish themselves call *Tir-nan-Og*.

In recent times, Ireland has seemed a poor relation of the industrialized countries. But archaeological finds show that it had a settled population 10,000 years ago, and that the Bronze Age technology was impressive. Chroniclers contrast the sturdy Irish-made weapons with those iron swords of British warriors, which had to be straightened out after each blow. Irish kings controlled the adjoining mainland and gave Scotland its name. From Iona an Irishman, Saint Columba, disciple of the great Saint Patrick, spread Christianity through northern Britain. *His* disciple, Columbanus, founded monasteries in heathen

France and Italy. What were Dark Ages to the rest of Europe was in fact a Golden Age of progress and enlightenment in Ireland.

In those days the inhabitants were divided into about 150 tribes, each with a king. Groups of kings rendered homage to four great kings. The latter dominated all Ireland and their kingdoms became the four 'provinces': Ulster in the north, Connaught in the west, Munster in the south west and Leinster in the south east. The names survive, though their significance today is more sentimental than administrative.

For a predominantly rural country, Ireland was fairly densely populated until disastrous potato harvests in the 1840s (the 'Hungry Forties') and subsequent mass emigration left whole counties desolate. Emigration, chiefly to America, has continued well into this century. By 1960 the population had sunk to 4,000,000 – less than half of what it had been in 1840. But in the past twenty years it has begun to rise again, particularly in the Republic.

The Republic of Ireland (it is no longer fashionable to speak of 'Eire') consists of the ancient provinces of Leinster, Munster and Connaught plus the three counties of Donegal, Cavan and Monaghan which are historically part of Ulster. The Republic is a parliamentary democracy, a member of the European Economic Community but not of NATO or the Commonwealth. Ireland also makes important contributions to the United Nations' peace-keeping forces.

Six northern counties which chose to remain outside the provisions of the Anglo-Irish treaty of 1921 (which brought the Irish Free State into existence) constitute Northern Ireland (not 'Ulster'). They are Derry, Tyrone, Fermanagh, Armagh, Down and Antrim and they are part of the United Kingdom of Great Britain and Northern Ireland.

The Royal Dublin Society's Spring Show (in May) at Ballsbridge attracts the world's show-jumping celebrities and big buyers as well as huge crowds of spectators. The demand from abroad for top-class Irish hunters and jumpers is nowadays almost as keen as the demand for Irish racehorses.

Dublin

In 1846, when the *Illustrated London News* launched its colour series on 'Great Capitals of the World', number one was Dublin. Perhaps the editor was an Irishman, nostalgic for Dublin's golden age of the 18th century. Only a sturdy patriot today would put Dublin at the head of capital cities. To the newcomer, advancing towards its heart from the Liffey quays or by Drumcondra from the airport, it rather resembles an overgrown, slightly neglected market town. Here and there a neo-Palladian building or a costly tower-block rises, but they seem to have been planted there by accident rather than design.

Some people are instantly charmed by the relaxed atmosphere, the smoky pubs and the demotic *élan* of a citizenry among whom the arts of conversation thrive. Others are initially confounded by the Dubliner's man-to-man familiarity, his irreverence towards authority (bogus traffic wardens, vendors of 'Disabled Driver' stickers) and his seemingly illogical order of priorities.

The city grew organically, died and sprang to life again. The Vikings, the first settlers, gave it its name, *Duibhlinn* meaning 'Blackpool' because of the peat-blackened River Liffey. The Gaels who came afterwards knew it as *Baile Atha Cliath* (the name seen on Dublin-postmarked letters), which means 'Town of the Hurdled Ford', a name derived from the act of an Ulster king who made a bridge of hurdles to cross the swollen Liffey. Fragments of those hurdles have been recovered from the river.

Dublin passed through the hands of Irish kings, Dermots of Leinster and Connors of Connaught, into those of the English king Henry II in 1172. For 750 years thereafter the

Previous page Liberty Hall, the Irish Transport & General Workers Union headquarters (1964) and James Gandon's neo-Palladian Custom House (1791) dominate the Liffey quays in Dublin.
Below Dublin University has only one college, founded by Queen Elizabeth I in 1591 and known the world over as Trinity College Dublin, or 'TCD'.

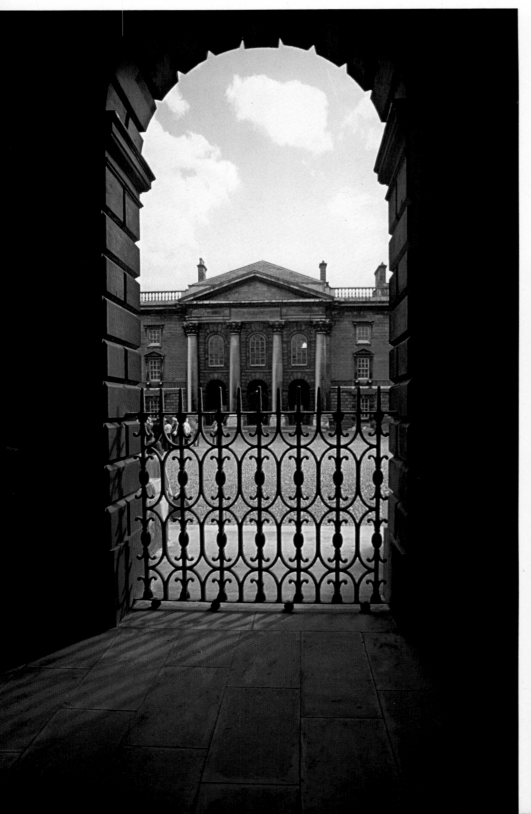

city was the power-base of the British in Ireland. Rebellions and religious struggles destroyed the picturesque abbeys and convents of Dublin's medieval piety. Out of the wretched hovels of Cromwell's devastation the elegant town houses, malls and piazzas of British expatriates arose. The Protestant Ascendancy was established, and the gulf between Anglo-Irish and native peasant widened. The principal university and the principal cathedral of this most Catholic of cities are Protestant foundations, memorials of that gulf.

An 18th-century banker and philanthropist called Luke Gardiner, created the handsome face of inner-city Dublin where, up to about 1800, Europe's most expensive painters, masons, stucco workers and craftsmen found lucrative commissions. Then came the Act of Union, by which Ireland became part of the United Kingdom. The rich merchants and landowners abandoned their Dublin mansions and went home to Britain. Crescents and terraces degenerated into slums. The condition of an impoverished urban population grew desperate. The Dublin of 'splendour built on squalor' became the 'dear, dirty Dublin' which most middle-aged inhabitants can remember, when horse-drawn traffic was common, barefooted children ran about the streets and beggars and ballad-singers haunted the Liffey quays. Town planning came too late to do more than complicate a street pattern apparently modelled on the monkish illuminations in the Book of Kells, where there are said to be as many as 185 convolutions and interlacings in a square inch of manuscript.

History has marred Dublin's beauty, but history has also given a zany twist to its life-style

Below Dublin's Mansion House, official residence of the Lord Mayor, was built in 1705. It is a Queen Anne house of simple dignity, not improved by its Victorian embellishments. The Round Room is open for public balls and concerts and here in January 1919 the first independent Irish parliament assembled.

and a raffish warmth to its citizens. Generous efforts have been made to save its more graceful aspects – the Georgian terraces, for example – but for every conservationist there appear to be two influential property speculators.

Among half a million Dubliners, the pure products of its splendours and miseries through the ages are found in the inhabitants of the Liberties. This area, originally sited just beyond the defended wall, covers both banks of the Poddle, a stream now confined underground which, readers of James Joyce's *Ulysses* will recall, 'hung out in fealty a liquid tongue of sewage' as the viceregal cavalcade passed by. Here is clustered the essence of working-class Dublin – bars galore, cut-price cake shops, old-clothes and pawnbrokers' shops, a garish Lourdes grotto, alleyway markets devoted to wallpaper and other homely commodities, warrens where small-scale local trades like silk-weaving and biscuit-making are carried on. (Until recently, one Liberties loner raised his own silkworms.) Mid-Victorian flagged streets are lined with one-storied cottages, tiny gar-

Above A landmark of central Dublin, the Halfpenny Bridge for foot passengers spans the Liffey. It takes its name from a toll formerly levied on those who used it.

Left The development of Georgian Dublin received its impetus from John Ensor, designer of Merrion Square for Lord Fitzwilliam. This detail of house fronts in Upper Mount Street gives a good idea of the restrained and elegant architecture of the terraces leading off the square.

Right 18th-century Dublin is today seen in all its tarnished glory in the quiet terraces of this district – Merrion, Fitzwilliam, Pembroke Streets and others. The cliff-like facades, plain exteriors faced with brick, painted doors and fan-lighted windows used to conceal an interior décor of luxury and extravagance. All the houses were speculatively built, most have now been converted to company offices and consulting rooms of law firms, doctors and stockbrokers.

Above The Gaelic, Viking and medieval shaping of Dublin is to be seen only in museums. The architecture of the city today is basically that of the mid-18th-century rococo boom town, refined by the Regency planners and overlaid by Victoriana. A Dublin citizen looking over the tangle of city-centre streets sees familiar aspects of a community which offers endless surprises for the stranger. On the south the mountains come to Dublin's doorstep. From Rathfarnharn in the suburbs it is a short drive on 'the military roads' to the rounded summits and heather moors of the Dublin hills. A tour of 48 km (30 m) takes in some of the best mountain scenery in Ireland.
Left For 700 years Dublin has supported two cathedrals, a stone's-throw apart, each built by an Anglo-Norman bishop. This is Saint Patrick's, the largest church in Ireland, situated in the Liberties quarter of the city.

dens and stout iron railings. On this section of the Dublin tourist trail, visitors may follow the blunderings of Robert Emmet, youthful leader of the 1803 rebellion. Deserted by his followers, he became trapped in the Liberties. Close by stood Kilmainham Gaol and the British garrison headquarters, both of which figure in local folklore. Ballads like *The Night Before Larry was Stretched* express the Liberties' morbid preoccupation with crime and punishment. Here too, in the strange juxtaposition typical of Dublin, stands the largest church in Ireland, St Patrick's Cathedral, with the grave of its one-time Dean, Jonathan Swift, author of *Gulliver's Travels* and other political satires.

The surviving grandeur, or grandiosity, of Dublin's architecture is found a few streets away. The impressively-cupola'd Four Courts, the Mansion House, Leinster House and Dublin Castle, the hospitals and Surgeons' College (Dublin was always famous for medicine), the old Parliament House (now the Bank of Ireland) and the green oases they look down on are relics of that age of elegance when society envisaged a 'fair city' fairer and nobler than was known to sweet Molly Malone in the song *Cockles and Mussels*. The smoke-blackened walls of Trinity College, an island of academic serenity embedded in a disorganized traffic flow, catch the visitor's eye. Rare gospel books, supreme among them the Book of Kells, kept therein are perhaps Ireland's richest treasures.

Millions of foreign visitors descend annually on Dublin, mostly from Britain and the United States, and they come for hundreds of different reasons. The James Joyce itinerary is a favourite – maps are provided and the journey ranges from Sandymount Tower on the south shore (the Joyce museum) to 'Howth Castle and Environs' on the north. Dublin is a festival city, with the accent on drama. It is an equestrian metropolis, whether for the ultra-modern sale-ring, the racecourses or the show-jumping arena. So successful are its tourist attractions that it is no surprise to find crowds flocking to a brewery (Guinness's, open to visitors every weekday), a cemetery (Glasnevin, where poets and patriots lie, adjoining luxurious botanical gardens) and a park (Phoenix Park, the broadest rural acreage within any European city).

There are few places to which visitors return so eagerly as to Dublin. It is a city which melts inhibitions, acting like a hall of distorting mirrors in which strangers delightedly recognize unexpected angles of themselves.

Close to Dublin there are other unusual attractions: a Japanese garden and a 122-metre (400-foot) cascade at Powerscourt; a falconry at Robertstown; a metropolis of 5,000-year-old dwellings at Newgrange; a canoe race down a torrential spate when reservoir waters are released into the Liffey; a mile-long chimney from an old lead factory to a hilltop near Bray; a highland pass in miniature on the 'military' road to the Dublin hills; a chair set daily for the unexpected guest at the dinner-table in Howth's feudal stronghold – those are merely samples of the innumerable off-beat touristic options with which this city of surprising character is ringed on its landward approaches.

Literary Ireland

'We are the greatest talkers since the Greeks,' said Oscar Wilde. Few will dispute the statement, for the pungency and poetry of everyday Irish speech are a constant amazement to the average tongue-tied user of the English language. If the Irish are so fluent in a language not their own, what must they be like in their ancestral tongue? Scholars say the ancient literature of Ireland is as rich as that of ancient Greece. To most, however, it is a closed book. The Irish mythology and the bardic tradition, transmitted by word of mouth, went underground long ago. At the end of the last century the Gaelic League attempted to revive it, and Douglas Hyde's monumental *History of Irish Literature* (1899) is actually in print again. But the great figures of Irish literature, including the 'Celtic Revivalists', have ordinarily written in English, aiming at the wider readership.

Irish writers have contributed elements to writing which the world finds attractive and impossible to imitate: a free-ranging imaginative fancy, a quirkiness and an irreverence, a tolerant view of the virtues and frailties of the human race. Jonathan Swift (1667–1745) Dean of Saint Patrick's Cathedral, Dublin, mingled innocent fun and bitter satire in books, letters and pamphlets, including the ever-popular *Gulliver's Travels*. Oliver Goldsmith (1728–1774) broke all the rules of dramatic composition yet in *The Vicar of Wakefield*, *She Stoops to Conquer* and *The Deserted Village*, he produced an outstanding novel, play and poem of a highly competitive age. His prolific younger contemporary, Richard Brinsley Sheridan (1751–1816) added those perennial favourites of drama groups, *The Rivals* and *The School for Scandal*.

For half a century George Bernard Shaw (1856–1950), critic and playwright, towered over the British theatre. He was writing masterpieces (*Back to Methuselah*, *Saint Joan*, *Pygmalion*) when nearly seventy and did not live to see *Pygmalion* become astonishingly successful as the musical *My Fair Lady*. A fellow Dubliner, Oscar Wilde (1854–1900), famous even among Irishmen as a conversationalist, wrote poems and perfectly-constructed plays. Though set firmly in a social scene long vanished, *The Importance of Being Ernest* and *Lady Windermere's Fan* continue to appeal to audiences the world over.

Irish poets and playwrights view life from a sharp angle. This is especially true of those of the 20th century, beginning

with W B Yeats (1865–1939) and J M Synge (1871–1909). A tale is told that Yeats in the course of his 'Celtic Revival' took a company of actors on tour in rural Ireland. They gave a play in a Connemara village and were greeted with silence. Eventually a farmer stood up and asked what the strangers were trying to do. Yeats explained what a play was, and the company went through the performance again. This time it was received with tumultuous applause.

Left to right Swift, Goldsmith, Sheridan, Wilde, Yeats (**above**), Joyce, Shaw – a pantheon of celebrities among the satirists, essayists, poets, novelists, playwrights and critics who for three centuries have helped confirm an opinion often voiced in literary circles that 'all the best English writers are Irishmen'.

Things are different now. Anyone walking into a village hall is liable to find a play in progress, or in rehearsal. There are the famous Abbey and Gate theatres, the Gaiety and Olympia, the Irish-language and experimental Peacock theatre and the 'pocket' Eblana under the central bus station, all in Dublin. Of provincial playhouses, the Opera and Everyman in Cork, the Gortycloona at Bantry, the Fo'castle in Galway City and the Talbot hotel (dinner theatre) at Wexford are keenly patronized. The Druid Lane Theatre Company of Galway has made a name for itself at international festivals abroad.

Dublin was shocked by drama which London and New York rapturously acclaimed: Synge's *Playboy of the Western World*, Sean O'Casey's *The Plough and the Stars* and *Juno and the Paycock*. The Irish, so ready to smile at themselves in real life, disliked seeing their foibles ridiculed on the stage. But today the Irish are enthusiasts for plebeian realism. Synge and Sean O'Casey (1884–1964) are forgiven.

George Moore (1852–1933) launched realism in the novel with *Esther Waters*. Ireland's (and according to some, the world's) most profound and original novelist is James Joyce (1882–1941). Echoes of *Ulysses* and *Finnegans Wake* are heard in the avant-garde plays of his protégé Samuel Beckett (*Waiting for Godot*). In our own times, Elizabeth Bowen (*The Last September*), Sean O'Faolain (*A Nest of Simple Folk*) and Frank O'Connor (*An Only Child*) have enriched the Irish novel with wit, pathos and wisdom. Irish capacity simultaneously to startle and amuse is demonstrated in the present-day work of Edna O'Brien (*The Country Girls*), which strikes a blow for feminism. A best-seller of the past decade has been James Plunkett's *Strumpet City*, an earthy tale of the Dublin of 70 years ago.

In realms of poetry, the pre-19th-century landmark is *Dark Rosaleen* (a personification of Ireland), attributed to Hugh O'Donnell, a 16th-century writer about whom little is known. There are charm and sugary sentiment in the *Irish Melodies* of Thomas Moore (1779–1852) and also poems of haunting beauty which, set to native airs, became the stock-in-trade of Irish lyric tenors (*The Harp that Once through Tara's Halls*). Ireland's only Nobel prize-winner is W B Yeats, but a number of bright stars rose after him, among them Louis MacNeice, Padraic Colum, Frank O'Connor and James Stephens. From County Meath came Lord Dunsany (1878–1960), also remembered for his brilliant short stories, and Francis Ledwidge, aged 30 when he was killed in the First World War, his genius unfulfilled.

Today there are signs of another Irish poetry renaissance. The younger talent has been led by two poets from Northern Ireland, W R Rogers and John Montague.

Leinster

1 Longford 2 Westmeath
3 Offaly 4 Meath 5 Louth
6 Dublin 7 Kildare 8 Laois
9 Carlow 10 Kilkenny
11 Wicklow 12 Wexford

Two Leinstermen came to blows over the question: which was the grandest scenic route of their province? One maintained it was Glendalough to Arklow, the other insisted it was Arklow to Glendalough.

Under Wicklow's brown turf, its bubbling torrents and bright splashes of yellow gorse, down the sylvan vales of Clara and Avoca, this grand, scenic route keeps company with the hurrying stream of the Avonmore. Travellers on the Wexford-Dublin railway may assess the quality of the scenery too: the builders of the track made a detour inland to Rathdrum, County Wicklow, crossing and recrossing the stream, as though to provide Ireland's transport company with a few subjects for posters.

Except for that detour, the trains hug the coastline, 'the rocky road to Dublin'. Arklow and Wicklow are touched at – two sleepy harbours where it always seems half-tide, with rusty coasting vessels heeled over in the silt. Nearing the capital, wayside halts become more frequent. Commuters get on, and the bucket-and-spade brigade get off at the platforms of such sparkling, sea-washed little towns as Greystones and Bray, County Wicklow, and Dalkey and Dun Laoghaire (pronounced 'Leary'), County Dublin. Dun Laoghaire is on the sea route from Holyhead in Wales. Ships calling there today bring tourists and automobiles to the Emerald Isle whereas in the past the visitors were invading armies and foreign governors. The archaic Irish settlements of Leinster are the inland towns like Athlone (County Westmeath), Kells and Navan (County Meath) and Kilkenny (County Kilkenny). The coastal towns like Drogheda (County Louth), Dublin itself, Wicklow and Arklow (County Wicklow) and Wexford (County Wexford) are of Viking origin.

The whole province bore the brunt of anglicization because Leinster's king, Dermot MacMurrough (or his faithless wife), thrown out for scandalous conduct, sought the aid of England's king. It was the year 1166. A century earlier, a Pope of Rome had authorized a Norman king to conquer England, and now another Pope gave Henry II permission to take and keep Ireland. The legal value of the document has been questioned, but Henry came and conquered. His lieutenant, Strongbow, entered Leinster by the back door of the Barrow-Nore estuary at Passage East (County Waterford), in 1170. He navigated by the light-tower on Hook Head, County Wexford – a light-tower which is now 1500 years old – and by the village of Crooke on the opposite shore. He would land his army, he swore, 'by Hook or by Crooke'; or so the story goes.

Within the decade another everyday expression was born. The invaders secured Dublin and parts of what are now Counties Louth, Meath and Kildare. Broken castle walls still punctuate the boundaries, and mark the outposts of that English-ruled enclosure or 'Pale'. The Irish population outside it, whose affairs were governed by tribal custom, at once became second-class citizens. They were described as being 'beyond the Pale'.

Leinster is historically the most populous province. Today, with just over a quarter of the Republic's area, it supplies more than half the members of the Irish *Dáil*, or House of Representatives. It is a land of waterways with five rivers and three canals which are pleasantly uncommercial. The rivers are the Boyne, Liffey, Slaney, Barrow and Nore; the canals are the Royal, Grand and Barrow. Typical scenery of the province is a shallow fertile valley, beef and dairy cattle grazing on small-acreage farms, a market town, a ruined chapel, a prehistoric fort or monument – all are linked by the canal or the languid, canal-like river, beside which a row of anglers can always be seen. The primitive monks loved these valleys, and so did the Anglo-Irish landowners. Deer-parks and mock-Gothic halls are found along with the

stones of Celtic Christianity.

The Boyne river is the epitome of Irish history. It seeps inauspiciously out of the water-meadows south of Trim, County Meath, where Saint Patrick built a church and the Norman conquerors overshadowed it with the 21-m (70-ft) walls of the stoutest stronghold in Ireland. The Boyne is also fed from the lakes and wayward streams of County Longford, and from the Bog of Allen, the treacherous quaking sponge which for so long soaked up Ireland's surplus water and rendered the midland counties useless for cultivation.

Fragments of a toy church at Ardagh, County Longford, recall Saint Mel, whom Patrick himself appointed bishop. (The ruin is still known as 'the cathedral'.) Oliver Goldsmith, poet and playwright, had good reason to remember Ardagh, for he mistook Ardagh House for an inn, and the chain of blunders which ensued are supposed to have given him the plot for the classic 18th-century comedy, *She Stoops to Conquer*. Goldsmith was on his way to his father's house at Lissoy at the time, a place now called Auburn (County Westmeath) because it was the 'sweet Auburn' of his *Deserted Village*, 'loveliest of the plain'.

Rivulets making at a gentle pace for the Boyne pass through Kells, now a small town of plain Georgian houses but in the past a holy place. It produced the illuminated *Book of Kells*,

Left and below Kells in County Meath (not to be confused with Kells in Kilkenny, another monastic foundation) is obligatory for people on ecclesiastical pilgrimages in Ireland. The place is memorable for the gorgeously illuminated gospel, the 8th-century *Book of Kells*, which came from Iona in Scotland and is now at Trinity College, Dublin. Scholars have studied this intricate work under the microscope for years without detecting a false line or irregular interlacement in the hand-made lettering of the holy text.

'the most beautiful book in the world', and housed the synod of 1152 which established the hierarchy of the church in Ireland. Streams trickle in from the Hill of Tara, scene of pagan mysteries and the crowning of Dark Age kings, where objects 6000 years old have been found. Both Kells and Tara are in County Meath, 'Royal Meath', on whose rolling pastures cattle-raising and hunting are the traditional occupations. Dublin barristers and stockbrokers, glimpsed going to the office in tweed jackets and black bowler hats, are almost certain to be looking forward to an afternoon with the Meath or Ballymacad hounds, or the Tara harriers. In County Meath, even the High Crosses in Celtic churchyards have hunting scenes carved on them; or so the story goes.

As the Boyne approaches the sea, relics of history and prehistory crowd closer to its banks. Here is Newgrange, County Meath, city of the megalithic dead. Here are Mellifont of the abbey and Monasterboice of the decorated crosses, both in County Louth. Above the river bridge at Slane, County Meath, is the cottage of Francis Ledwidge the poet (killed in Flanders, 1917), and above the wooded slope rise the pseudo-medieval towers of Slane Castle, one of numerous stately homes on the Irish Georgian Society's circuit. At the mouth of the river stands Drogheda of brutal Cromwellian memory, with the shrivelled head of Oliver Plunkett on display in its uninspiring main-street cathedral. Plunkett, hanged in 1681, was canonized in 1975.

North of Drogheda, next door to the Northern Ireland border, Dundalk is lively, especially when music and drama groups descend on the town from many foreign countries for the annual Maytime Festival (last week of May).

The National Stud at Kildare, on the rolling heathland of the Curragh (2000 hectares, 5000 acres) is a state enterprise, the breeding of bloodstock being a vital Irish industry. About 1500 horses are stabled in and around the small town of Kildare, which also has non-equestrian attractions: the remains of a 6th-century monastery of Saint Brigid, which housed both monks and nuns; the diocesan centres of a Catholic and a Protestant bishop; and (close to the Stud) a famous garden laid out in 1906 by the Japanese landscape master Eito.

This county town of Louth is a centre for the Cooley Hills, the Republic's answer to the North's mountains of Mourne. Campers and picnic parties occupy the springy turf which is steeped in mythical symbolism, with tales every Irish child is brought up on, regarding Cuchulain the boy hero, Queen Maeve or Mab and the Red Bull, Finn MacCool the giant and his mastiff Bran.

The peacefully-winding canals, reed-fringed and kingfisher-haunted, passing under humped bridges clothed in creeper and moss, are the routes best suited for a foray into Leinster's inland counties of Westmeath, Offaly, Laois and Kildare, if the visitor has time to spare. The Royal (now derelict) and the Grand canals were the first in the British Isles, the main arteries of a system of waterways designed to connect Dublin with the far west.

The Royal, or what is left of it, goes out from Dublin by Leixlip ('Salmon Leap'), County Kildare, where the salmon have had to take an artificial route since the power station was built on the Liffey at Leixlip waterfall; by Maynooth, the pontifical university for Ireland's priesthood and to Mullingar in the lakeland area of Westmeath. A hamlet near Mullingar bears the name Pass-if-you-can – souvenir of an ambush of the English garrison in 1642. Westward towards Athlone, three separate hills each proclaim themselves the mathematical centre of Ireland. The likeliest is Ushnagh (184m, 602ft), once held by Brian Boru in a gesture of defiance against royal Tara. Despite that modest height, 20 of Ireland's 32 counties and all the midland boglands are visible from the summit.

Starting from Dublin's dockland, the Grand canal passes north of the Curragh of Kildare. Curragh means 'marsh', but this is a breezy, furzy heath devoted to horse-racing and breeding (the home of the National Stud and many private stud-farms) and to the training of the Irish Army in barracks which formerly housed the British military establishment.

On its way to Tullamore, noted for whiskey and boatyards and for being consistently among the 'cleanest town' award-winners, the canal traverses bog country, once densely forested, but now bleak and desolate. There was a time when the barges, piled high with sods (bricks) of turf (peat), made their sluggish way to Dublin from these midland bogs. On the city wharves the slum-dwellers, shawled and shoeless in the rain, would bargain for the fuel, three sods for a penny. 'Here's the dry turf, here's the dry bog-a-wood, buy the chips to light the fire, maids' – those days are gone and now the Tullamore-Shannon Harbour-Kilcormac triangle (County Offaly) looks from the canal like a sheet of brown cardboard, with the Peat Board's combine harvesters crawling over it, skimming, chopping, stockpiling and despatching by the trainload Ireland's prime raw energy material.

Dying villages live again as tourism rejuvenates the canals. Robertstown, County Kildare, offers a 'Canal Festa' every weekend in July and August, with floating banquets, swimming races, balloon ascents and the Falconry of

Ireland. Daingean, County Offaly, is once more on the map; so is Portlaoise, County Laois, (pronounced 'leash'). More than four centuries ago, Queen Mary of England ('Bloody Mary') decreed that those towns should be named Philipstown and Maryborough, the former in honour of her husband Philip of Spain. They never prospered, and neither did their counties, which before independence were called King's and Queen's.

The Offaly-Laois border curls round the Slieve Bloom mountains, one of Ireland's few inland ranges. The lower ground was bog, negotiable only on causeways where skeletons and Stuart coins have been found. Pass of the Plumes commemorates an old bog path where Lord Essex's well-dressed army suffered annihilation in 1599, and their feathered caps were scattered in the swamp. But sometimes a causeway ended at a secret monastery. One such is Saint Comghan's at Killeshin, County Carlow, a refuge of scholars for 600 years, which was trampled into the bog by Norman invaders in 1077, then in our own times salvaged and given a face-lift.

Portlaoise is on the infant Barrow river and Killeshin is close to the Barrow canal. River and canal, picturesquely intertwined, head southward to the sea via Carlow (County Carlow), once a strategic crossing-point and now – since the waterways were reopened to small boat navigation – a mecca for sailing and motor boating enthusiasts. Landmarks of the route include a huge prehistoric portal at Kernanstown (County Carlow) – the roofslab alone weighs 100 tons – and the ruin of Sleaty Cathedral (near Carlow town), whose 7th-century bishop dictated the *Life of Saint Patrick*, the source of almost all that is known about the patron saint of Ireland.

The Nore river, rich in salmon, comes down from County Kilkenny and combines with the Barrow at New Ross, County Wexford, to make a 32-km (20-mile) fiord to the sea. Jerpoint near Thomastown (County Kilkenny) is the Nore's principal ecclesiastical relic, and Kilkenny Castle, seat of the medieval Leinster seneschals, is its most complete fortress. A smooth black stone, quarried near the town, gives Kilkenny the name of 'Marble City'. It is a go-ahead place. Its Design Workshops are a model of community craft projects, its archaeology and folklore are vividly displayed in the complex of ancient buildings called Rothe House. Kilkenny City has an annual Arts Week (end of August), second only to Dublin's, an annual Air Fair (celebrating the fact that the first man to fly across the Irish Sea was from Kilkenny) and annual archery, golf and ballooning championships. Agricultural industries are booming and the district is popular with foreign companies seeking to establish themselves in Ireland. At work and play, Kilkenny disposes of the myth that the Irish are a lackadaisical race.

Foreign accents, especially American ones, are heard in the huge park at New Ross, which is stocked with the most comprehensive collection of trees and shrubs known to arboriculturists. The park is dedicated to John F Kennedy, and was set up during the wave of adulation which hit Ireland after the President's assassination. New Ross is the ancestral Kennedy village. The cottage at Dunganstown from which the Kennedy forebears emigrated to Boston USA is once again inhabited by a family of the name of Kennedy.

New Ross, for the tourist, has the additional attraction of being a terminus of delightful estuary voyages and the self-drive cruising holidaymaker may travel all the way to Dublin on the meandering canals, switching from the Barrow to the Grand at Monasterevin. The busiest port of County Wexford is on Ireland's south-eastern extremity at Rosslare. There are automobile-carrying connections with France as well as England and Wales.

Wexford town remains the chief touring centre, with its medley of scenes attracting great attention. There are the quays and main streets which make up in inordinate length what they lack in width; the maritime museum (situated in a former lightship) and the plain old theatre, friendly and unpretentious as a village hall, to which every October the critics and music-lovers of all the nations come to hear Europe's famous singers and orchestras perform rarely-heard operas.

The Slaney river, springing from the Wicklow hills and rippling down through birch-wood and farmland, waters a marsh country on Wexford's doorstep, outstanding for the number and variety of its wildfowl.

The Slaney runs south, the Liffey – rising in the same hills – forces a passage through gorges, plunges down rapids and then swings to the north, spending its youthful exuberance in Dublin's suburbs. The romantic route over the Wicklow hills, skirting the sources of those two rivers, is the so-called Military Road from Rathfarnham, south Dublin. This road did not exist until the Wexford rebels threatened the capital in 1798 and an army had to be deployed to oppose them. Laragh, County Wicklow, site of the government barracks of that campaign, commands five glens with slender ribbons of road passing beside streams and glistening rocks. Down Glendasan ran Saint Kevin's Road, a trail which the young saint blazed in about 600 AD, traces of which can still be found in places. It comes out at Glendalough ('Glen of Two Lakes'), where Kevin dug out his cell.

He was an Irish Saint Francis, who lived ages before Assisi was thought of, and was a friend to dumb creatures. When he was hungry, a blackbird laid her eggs in his hand. When he thirsted, a wild deer offered herself to be milked. Kevin was not lonely for long. Seven churches rose on the lake shore, and modern scholars have learned much from the inscriptions on their pillars and cross-slabs. It is

Left Kilkenny has been described as Ireland's most rewarding city – a provincial town with arcaded streets, cathedral, castle and Round Tower, carefully-restored houses and high-quality design workshops, sophisticated industries, excellent fishing . . . and above all an air of continuing history past, present and future. **Below** The interior dimensions of Kilkenny Castle reflect the grandeur of the Norman pile. Even today one shrinks a little, when driving past this seat of the once-powerful Butler family.

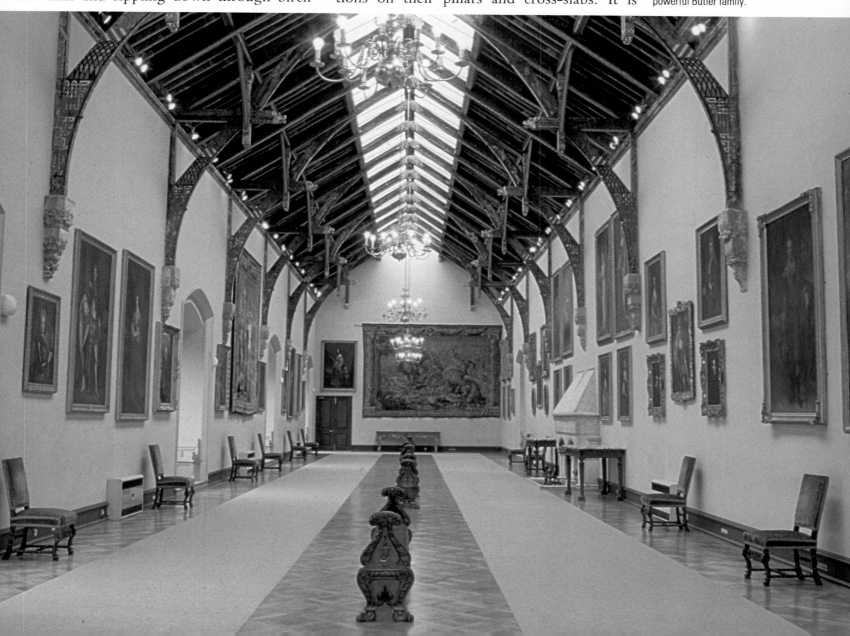

astonishing that anything survived. Before the 12th century ended, the monastery had been nine times burned down, four times pillaged and once devastated by flood. Yet the monks came back and, at least since the era of the most distinguished abbot, Saint Lawrence O'Toole (he became archbishop of Dublin in 1162), the monastic tradition has remained pure and unbroken and the archictecture intact.

Glendalough to Arklow, Arklow to Glendalough – pilgrims and excursionists come and go in both directions and still the 'grandest scenic route' debate is not resolved. The antiquities of Glendalough cast the more powerful spell. They seem to sleep in a permanent Celtic twilight. We can hardly make out the original plan of them, but along the lake shore we find ourselves speaking in whispers, as though in a cathedral.

Left Wexford, a Norse foundation, is the nearest town to Wales, but the cross-channel boats come in at Rosslare, 21 km (13 miles) away. Wexford boasts the driest, sunniest weather and some of the tiniest streets and shops in Ireland. Incongruous shop signs indicate the versatility of the provincial Irish tradesman.
Main picture First historical mention of Carlow is in 1180, when an invading Anglo-Norman general built a castle to command the ford over the River Barrow. The river's banks, however, are littered with ancient monuments and tales of Gael and Celt. These, and the charms of two serene pastoral waterways (river and canal), make Carlow a popular base for holidaymakers afloat.

The Holy Places

The ancient Romans ignored Ireland. Consequently, when Christianity took root, it flourished undisturbed and the visible signs of the faith – chapels, crosses, manuscripts – survived. As time went by, communities of preaching monks developed, each in his own cell. Free of the discipline which increasingly authoritative popes and bishops imposed on other countries, the monks founded their own small monasteries and went on their own missionary journeys.

Many holy places of Ireland have been in a state of picturesque ruin for nearly a thousand years, from the time when on account of their wealth and importance, they were the targets of Viking invaders. **Left** The cathedral at Ardfert, County Kerry. **Below** Cloisters of Quin Friary near Ennis, County Clare.

Right Round Towers of Irish monasteries were belfries and places of refuge for the monks and, all too frequently, lightning conductors. One which has survived nine centuries intact is this finely-cut, decorated Tower of Ardmore, County Waterford. It adjoins the ruins of Saint Declan's church.

They came into contact with the world of classical learning and produced copies of the standard Latin texts. Places like Clonmacnois and Glendalough became famous academic centres. Ireland's patron saint, Patrick, by birth a Briton but taken to Ireland as a slave, established his church in about 440 AD at Armagh in Ulster. His successors sailed the seas: Columcille, called Columba, to Scotland, Brendan possibly to America, Colman, called Columbanus, to France and Italy, Aidan to Lindisfarne in Northumbria. Travelling monks made converts all over Europe. St Gallen in Switzerland is named after Gall, an Irish monk. The oldest churches of Salzburg in Austria and Würzburg in Bavaria are dedicated to the Irish monks Fergal and Cilian who took Christianity to those lands.

In honour of the 6th- and 7th-century holy travellers, the Roman Catholic world has bestowed on Ireland the title 'Isle of Saints'. For every one who travelled abroad, scores remained at home. Insignificant ruins all over the country perpetuate the names of local, obscure but quite genuine saints who were both male and female: Gobnat, Comgall, Finnian, Samthann, Lurach, Seanan, Finbarr, Mochuar, Mel, Domangard and hundreds more.

In other lands in the middle ages, emperors and kings expressed their piety or sought to save their souls by building splendid cathedrals. Irishmen lacked the skill to compete. The most ambitious complex, on Saint Patrick's Rock at Cashel in County Tipperary, is interestingly decorated but extremely modest in size. Later on, the Protestant Ascendancy prevented Ireland from acquiring the large monasteries and sumptuous baroque churches found in most Catholic countries. Through good times and bad, the tradition remained monastic rather than episcopal.

In country districts, religion is still a part of everyday life. Local saints are venerated and 'pattern' (pilgrimage) days see large crowds assembled for picturesque ceremonies. A simple Celtic cross in a churchyard or a few sunken stones outlining a vanished priory's foundations have their stories and legends of saintly heroes and heroines. To their neighbourhoods they are eloquent, and from such places have come the artistic marvels of primitive monasticism: figured stone carvings on the High Crosses, jewelled ornaments like the Ardagh chalice (Dublin, National Museum) and painted gospels like the Book of Kells (Dublin, Trinity College).

Mellifont Abbey (County Louth) is perhaps the most charming of medieval ecclesiastical ruins. It was the first Cistercian abbey, founded in 1140. It gave birth to Bective (County Meath), Boyle (County Roscommon), Monasternenagh (County Limerick), Baltinglass (County Wicklow) and a host of smaller establishments. In the grounds of Ashford Castle (Cong, County Mayo), former seat of the Guinness family and now a hotel, stands the Augustinian ruin where Rory O'Connor, last High King of Ireland, was buried in 1189. At nearby Mayo, an abbey called Mayo of the Saxons was already 500 years old at that date. It was founded by Saint Colman, and tradition says that King Alfred the Great studied there.

'Monaster' in an Irish place-name denotes a religious settlement. Monasterboice (County Louth) has little of its 6th-century foundation to show, but the village is famous for its intricately-embroidered High Crosses and what is left of its 61-m (200-ft) Round Tower. (The Round Towers, a feature of early Irish churches, were a kind of belfry, detached from the main building.)

Monasterevin ('Eimhin's monastery') in County Kildare was transformed, like many stone buildings, into a private house – home of the Earls of Drogheda and afterwards of Count John MacCormack the operatic tenor.

The most visited monastery in Ireland is Saint Kevin's 6th-century retreat in Glendalough (County Wicklow) – partly for a tall Round Tower which has worn well but chiefly for its lovely setting in the Glen of Two Lakes. The fathers of the Church had an eye for natural beauty. At his 7th-century monastery of Aghadoe (County Kerry), of which only ruins are left, Saint Fionan Lobhar, 'Fionan the leper', had the consolation of magnificent views over Killarney's mountains. Close at hand, the walls of Muckross Abbey in the great Muckross demesne overlook a panorama of the Killarney lakes.

Clonmacnois (County Offaly) was a city of monasteries and a graveyard of kings. Ballintubber (County Mayo), Jerpoint and Kells (County Kilkenny), Holycross (County Tipperary), Duleek (County Meath) and Devenish (County Fermanagh) are among abbeys of outstanding historic interest. Of the most ancient and venerated sites, the chapel of Saint Finbarr, to whom Cork Cathedral is dedicated, at Gougane Barra (County Cork), and the 4th-century oratory of Gallarus near Ballyferriter (County Kerry), quaint in design and perfect in tranquillity, are high on the ecclesiastical pilgrim's list.

Faughart (County Louth) has a shrine and precious relics of Saint Brigid, patroness of Ireland, who was thought to have been born there. Downpatrick (County Down) has fragments of a church attributed to Saint Patrick himself, reputedly buried there along with Saint Brigid and Saint Columba in what is now the cathedral crypt.

Munster

1 Clare 2 Kerry 3 Limerick
4 Cork 5 Tipperary
6 Waterford

Previous page Tramore harbour
and Lady Elizabeth's Cove, a venue
for sea-bathing, skin-diving and
boating on the Munster coast near
Waterford.

The ragged edges of the wildest, and at the same time mildest, of coastlines define the south-western land mass called Munster. It is sparsely inhabited, except in the tourist season, with only half the population of Leinster (but twice that of Connaught). Here, however, are found Cork and Limerick, the busiest cities outside Dublin and Belfast.

Much of Munster consists of tapering promontories, combed out by the heavy seas and south-westerly gales of the Atlantic. Each of these separate little lands have in common with the others a profusion of wild flowers. Fuchsia and gorse, bluebell and saxifrage, arbutus and orchis grow prodigiously because of the exceptionally warm (and wet) winters and the sight of them is startling to those who have seen such plants only under cultivation. The sea cliffs are frightening in their rugged grandeur. One can almost credit the legends that giants trimmed them with colossal axes.

The novelist Thackeray placed the countryside between Kenmare and Dingle Bay among the world's wonders for scenery. J M W Turner considered the sunsets the finest on earth. Sir Walter Scott, though strongly prejudiced in favour of Scotland, admitted the seascapes to be the grandest he had viewed.

Such admiring superlatives are at least partly brought about by the suddenness with which the panoramic south west bursts upon the traveller after a journey through pleasantly pastoral, but essentially rather monotonous, hinterland scenes.

Munster's one landlocked county is Tipperary. But even that has a share in Lough Derg, an inland sea. Tipperary town lies in the Golden Vale, or Golden Vein – nothing to do with the

precious minerals sought in hills to the north, but golden for its fertility. South of the county town the road climbs the shoulder of Galtymore (920m, 3018ft), Ireland's third highest mountain after Carrantuohill (Kerry) and Lugnaquilla (Wicklow). Tipperary was the ancestral town of William Hazlitt the essayist and Eugene O'Neill the American playwright. It is said that the English composer of the famous marching song, *It's a Long Way to Tipperary*, never visited the place and did not know where it was.

Tipperary has escaped violent history. Not so Cashel, a straggling market town under a great rock. The name Cashel suggests *Castellum*, a Roman camp – something virtually unknown in Ireland. From this rock Brian Boru (from whom all O'Briens are descended) defied the O'Neills, kings of Tara, and briefly unified all Ireland. But the fortress has been a cathedral for the past 700 years. The ruins which survive are those of the ecclesiastical, not the political, capital of Munster.

One of Ireland's gentlest rivers, the Suir, flows down from the Golden Vale to Waterford by way of Clonmel ('Honey Meadow') and Carrick-on-Suir, formerly a stronghold of the Butlers, Earls of Carrick and Ormond, all-powerful in Tudor times. At Waterford the river is a deep-sea channel. Container loads on the quays are labelled for exotic destinations, but cattle, bacon and crystal glass are the county's chief contributions and Waterford town behind the long harbour front is a very provincial pattern of little shops and cafés. This being Ireland, there must be some cultural incongruity amongst this provinciality, and there is – the Theatre Royal. A replica of La Scala Milan, it stands nobly in its rags of red plush,

Below left The ruined cathedral on the Rock of Cashel, County Tipperary, occupies the site of a royal palace and stronghold of Brian Boru, High King of Ireland. **Below** Blarney entered the language as a synonym for smooth talk. The castle, near Cork, is more properly a tower house, a type of residence favoured by Irish chieftains from about 1500 AD. More than 300 such 'castles' survive in County Cork, and nearly 400 in County Limerick next door.

Left Before the city of Cork opened her quays to deepwater vessels it was at Cobh on an island in Cork's great landlocked harbour that the fleets of all the nations lay. In its 19th-century heyday Cobh was called Queenstown, after Queen Victoria. The first steamship to cross the Atlantic – the *Sirius* in 1838 – sailed from this quay, and the British Navy maintained a base here until 1937. Cobh is today the headquarters of the world's oldest yacht club which, in republican Ireland, still clings to its original name, Royal Cork. The neo-Gothic cathedral of Saint Colman, designed by Pugin, towers over the waterfront.

Above On a summer day, Munster's south-western inlets are deceptively calm. In winter storms they live up to the name of this one: Roaring Water Bay.

gold leaf and baroque decoration, a memento of Irish opera's heyday.

Most memorable of 'those tiresome works', as George Bernard Shaw called them, 'which have for so long enjoyed the favour of the lower classes' were Balfe's *The Bohemian Girl* (1843), Wallace's *Maritana* (1845) and Benedict's *The Lily of Killarney* (1862). They were extremely popular with the Victorians.

Waterford was a cradle of Irish opera. William Vincent Wallace was born there, in what is now the Maritana guest-house. He led the life of a typical devil-may-care Irishman: stole a nun from a convent and married her, emigrated to Australia and ran off with her sister, became successively a bushranger, sheep-farmer and sailor. In the South Seas he joined a mutiny, in New Zealand he narrowly missed being eaten by cannibals, in India he was mauled by a tiger, in Peru he went to war, in Chile he was injured in an earthquake. Through all those adventures a violin was his passport; but he did not play well enough to earn a living when he eventually reached London.

Instead he sat down and in six weeks composed *Maritana*. It was the musical sensation of the decade. Tastes have since changed, but a few of its arias and duets – *Let Me Like a Soldier Fall, Maritana, Wildwood Flower, Scenes that are Brightest* and *There is a Flower that Bloometh* – are not disdained by the great tenors and sopranos of today.

Irish to the last, Wallace squandered his money in reckless speculations and foolish generosity and died penniless. His widow lived miserably in a Dublin slum, giving piano lessons. His son entered the poorhouse and his two stepsons committed suicide.

Waterford's musical traditions persist. Pop singers Val Doonican and Gilbert O'Sullivan are both natives of the town. An annual Light Opera Festival (October) at the Theatre Royal is a sort of tribute to William Vincent Wallace.

'Scenes that are Brightest' might describe the chain of seaside resorts which connects Counties Waterford and Cork. Some, like Tramore, Ardmore and Youghal (pronounced 'Yawl') glitter a little harshly in summer. Others, notably Dunmore East and Clonea, offer simplicity and serenity.

Cork is Ireland's largest county, 161km (100 miles) from eastern border to western tip. Cork city spreads over the head of an enclosed haven in which, despite big islands, half the world's fleets might hide. At their base on Haulbowline Island the little ships of the Irish Navy look quite lost. Cobh ('Cove'), formerly known as Queenstown, was a commercial port and main western headquarters of the British Fleet when

The ancient fishing port of Baltimore, close to the extreme tip of a remote south-western peninsula, gave its name to Baltimore, Maryland, USA: a great city of which the Irish, significantly, soon took political control. Baltimore in County Cork has been noted for 300 years as a school for boat-builders. Nowadays its boatyard builds and repairs yachts and its fishermen provide sea-angling excursions for visitors. Baltimore's history is as tempestuous as the ocean which thunders against its promontory. In 1537 the little town went to war with Waterford over a confiscated ship. A hundred years later occurred the notorious Sack of Baltimore, when pirates from Algeria snatched most of the inhabitants and sold them into slavery. The 19th-century dream of western outposts like Baltimore – of becoming a transatlantic packet station – remained a dream.

Ireland was a viceroyalty of the United Kingdom. James Joyce in *Ulysses* refers to 'Queenstown harbour full of Italian ships' and the names of some Cork districts – Ringabella, Montenotte, Tivoli – recall that venerable trading link.

Unremarkable historically and architecturally, Cork is a good shopping town and a progressive music and drama centre with an internationally-recognized Film Festival (annually in June). The city has a reputation for a high liquor consumption, but we are still in Ireland and must therefore not be surprised that, incongruously, Cork's most impressive statue commemorates a crusading teetotaller. Father Theobald Mathew, after whom a city quay is also named, had a tremendous success (but not a lasting one) early in the 19th century with his temperance campaigns.

In the same era another Cork priest, Francis Mahoney, wrote from exile in Rome the doggerel lines which mid-Victorian drawing-rooms wept over: *The Bells of Shandon*. Shandon bells still play every evening from the church in the crowded, hilly quarter of Cork. For a small fee, visitors can play the bells themselves.

Cork county is a land of castles. The best-known, Blarney, a gaunt ruin 8km (5 miles) from the city, bestows the gift of a ready tongue on all who manage to wriggle backwards through a slit near the top of a tower and kiss a marked stone. The tale goes that Queen Elizabeth I coined the word 'blarney', meaning plausible talk, after she had demanded that the castle be yielded to her. The owner had agreed, then spun out the years with endless excuses for not complying with the order.

Round ancient manor houses flit the shadows of Edmund Spenser the Elizabethan poet, William Penn the Quaker who gave his name to Pennsylvania and Sir Walter Raleigh, who is said to have planted the first potato outside the New World in a garden at Youghal. The extraordinary success of that vegetable in Ireland's soil made it for 200 years the staple diet of the peasantry. When the crops of the late 1840s failed, lack of the indispensable potato

was the beginning of Ireland's famine and mass emigration to England and America.

The string of beaches, bathing stations and fishing harbours continues. Kinsale, a flourishing sea-angling centre, clings to its antiquated ways on the tortuous inlet behind the Old Head of Kinsale. The townsfolk are occasionally seen in a black hooded cloak, reminiscent of the Maltese *faldetta*, but the rest of their picturesque costume is nowadays visible only in museums. (Note that, where most museums are open on weekdays and closed on Sundays, certain County Cork museums are open only on Sundays.)

A town centre sign indicates English Camp, O'Neill's Camp and French Prison. This says something about Kinsale's stormy past as a backdoor route for invasions of the British Isles. Britain's ex-king, James II, landed here in 1688 to try to regain his throne. He was defeated on the Boyne, north of Dublin, by his successor, William of Orange.

The bays and headlands are desolate, but they figure prominently on mariners' charts. Balti-

more, a lonely township, looks over the archipelago of Roaring Water Bay to Mizen Head. Pastel-shaded Ballydehob surveys Cape Clear and the Fastnet Rock. In 1631, Barbary corsairs raided this coast and carried off half the population of Baltimore and months went by before anyone knew about it. They were emigrant descendants of the survivors who founded a more prosperous Baltimore in Maryland, USA.

It is bleak all the way to Bantry, but there the traveller picks up a lively tourist trail, the 'Prince of Wales' route to Glengarriff and Killarney. Fuchsia, palm, fern, bamboo and Lebanon cedar abound. The physical beauties, great and small, of the 'Kingdom' of Kerry are hard to exaggerate, from the majestic sweep of Macgillycuddy's Reeks (Carrantuohill, 1041m, 3414ft, is Ireland's highest summit) to the rare tropical lichens at the water's edge.

County Kerry limps along a few decades behind the rest of the world – unless that is merely the astute face it presents to lovers of the quaint and nostalgic. Milk-churns rattle at

sleepy level-crossings. Undersized mokes and their wizened drivers stand askew on a steep cobbled street, waiting for the creamery or the pub to open. In the village church a jam-jar of wild flowers decorates the Virgin's alcove. Kerry, a compendium of all that is naïve and childlike about Ireland, is a *Gaeltacht* (Irish-speaking) enclave, a land of short fast rivers, miniature bays and caverns, little byways, little islands, sly and whimsical toytowns – set amid vast ocean prospects, generous expanses of pure pale sand and formidable ascents and descents through the 'Gaps' in the Reeks.

Modest in construction but rich in scenery, the castles of an improbable nobility are dotted about. If the name of the Macgillycuddy of the Reeks sounds bizarre, it is some consolation that no feudal baron took his title from mountain loughs which have names like Derreenadavodia and Eekenohoolikeagaun.

The county seat of Kerry is Tralee, a small bacon-curing town. Like nearby Killorglin of Puck Fair fame, Tralee erupts once a year in a festival (end of August). Race meetings, concerts, battles of flowers and street entertainments build up to the Rose of Tralee finals, a beauty contest frequently won by an American Doctor of Philosophy. The old song says ''Twas not her beauty alone that won me' and it needs brains as well to win the judges' approval.

This small town was once railhead for delightful train rides. The narrow-gauge Dingle track (modern roads follow the route) set off towards a mysterious other-world of menhirs and beehive huts. Until Hollywood came to Dingle to put it on the map with the movie *Ryan's Daughter*, that westernmost town in Europe had scarcely seen foreigners; now it is overwhelmed by them. The Dingle peninsula and the off-shore Blaskets (revealed through the

Below left Tourists who do not know Ireland usually go there in search of scenic beauty, and most of them go where scenery is abundant and heavily-publicized: the lakes of Killarney and the mountains which are the awesome backcloth to them fulfill these requirements. Here the tourist symbols of the Emerald Isle cluster thickly: the shamrock, the souvenir shillelagh, the side-car or jaunting car – not forgetting the car's driver, a stage Irishman with a fund of improbable stories to explain the natural curiosities of the route.

autobiographical sketches of Maurice O'Sullivan and blind Peig Sayers) are something of a cult region for seekers after *Tir-nan-Og*, the land of lost content.

Another railway went from Tralee to the far tip of Iveragh, the peninsula west of Killarney. Traces are visible on the Ring of Kerry road near Killorglin, Glenbeigh, Kells and Caherciveen. Where the line ended, a ferryboat went over to a neat little amphitheatre of black and white houses on Valentia Island. This is Knightstown, named for the Knight of Kerry, another potentate who traces his ancestry to a feudal baron of Norman times.

The railway was meant to be part of a grand inter-continental expressway, a 'short sea' route from London to America via Holyhead and Dublin. Valentia Island and Galway City had advanced arguments for becoming the chief transatlantic steam-packet port, each claiming to be the nearest harbour to America. Accurate measurements confirmed Valentia Island's claim: from Knightstown to Nova Scotia it is only 3452km (2145 miles). Daniel O'Connell the Liberator, a silver-tongued Kerryman, proposed the grand railway scheme and the British government, pursuing a policy known as 'killing Irish Home Rule with kindness', adopted it. But the Irish counties could not agree on a line of route from Dublin and when O'Connell died in 1847 the line and the 'short sea' dream died too.

A railway of sorts came into being. It took mackerel and shellfish up to the Dublin markets and it brought down meteorologists to Valentia's important observatory and weather station – the Tigh na gCupan or 'House of Cups' as local people called it, from the spinning anemometers on its roof. The line closed a few years ago and its route now makes a long-distance

Below right Travellers approach the summit of the Gap (mountain pass) of Dunloe in MacGillicuddy's Reeks, a range which contains Ireland's highest peak. The narrow winding track, unsuitable for automobiles but much trafficked in the season by walkers, ponies and side-cars, leads southwards from Beaufort Bridge near Killarney. The cottage of Kate Kearney, 19th-century belle of the mountains, who used to fortify travellers with illicit whiskey, stands at the northern end of the route.

nature trail for energetic walkers between Tralee and Reenard Point. There is now a road bridge to Valentia Island.

North-east out of Kerry the first sizeable town is Limerick, an ancient strategic strong-point at the Shannon's lowest crossing-point. Like Dublin, the city has been in the thick of history from Norse times. It is noted for delicate lace (*guipure*) made by nuns, and is a good touring centre for the Shannon basin and the wilder shores of County Clare.

At Moher on the Clare coast the Atlantic wall presents its greatest bulk and height to the ocean (204m, 668ft). The district is a mass of curiosities. Liscannor, birthplace of John Holland (1841–1914) who invented the submarine, has the Pope for its parish priest and is renowned for the dignity of its religious processions. The black cobblestones of Liscannor's foreshore, rolled smooth by wave action, were sold to pave the streets of English Liverpool.

On the same shore, boatmen may be seen in shapeless homespun clothes with thick square trouser-seats, loading their purchases – apple tarts, darning needles, firewood, possibly a small black blindfolded bull – into a curragh, a flimsy lath-and-tarred-canvas boat, for a hazardous 14½-km (9-mile) voyage. They are Aran islanders, said to be the last true peasantry in Europe.

Lahinch (County Clare) has the oldest golf-course in Ireland, laid out by Black Watch soldiers based at Limerick when Napoleon was alive. At Moneen's ruined church near Carrigaholt the 'movable Ark' is kept – a big box which served as a mobile church between high and low tidemarks, that being the only place where the law of the Anglican Ascendancy could not interfere with the Mass.

Kerry has its tropical plants, but this district can offer both Arctic and alpine. In limestone gulleys on the Burren plateau, near Lisdoon-varna, gentians and various rare species thrive.

Right Frail boats of lath and tarred canvas, commonly called curraghs, still transport goods and passengers from the mainland to the Aran Islands. For the visitor apprehensive of primitive modes of transport there are motor boats from Liscannor in Clare and Salthill near Galway, and light aircraft from Oranmore, Galway.

Below Atlantic billows and westerly gales have sculpted the coastline of Kerry from old red sandstone and lime rock. On gentler slopes, such as this one at Finan's Bay, a mixture of sunny skies and copious rainfall brings heavy crops of cereals and dairy produce. Kerry is renowned for cattle, donkeys and dogs (the Kerry blue). In a Percy French poem the solitary reaper and the herdsman pause to watch the emigrant ship pass down the bay, with loved ones on board who will never return to their homes.

Trotting to the Fair

In the continuing drama of Irish life, the horse plays a crucial role. Visitors quickly learn how important he is. Their first view of him is often the rear end, between the shafts of a gypsy caravan – a type of holiday which Ireland pioneered and other countries copied. 'You take two friends and come back with three,' the slogan says – the third being the horse.

Post-trekking, or long-distance pony-trekking, is also popular, especially in the west, an extended trail ride with escort and overnight accommodation at farmhouses. Equestrian enthusiasts can visit the National Stud at the Curragh, County Kildare, and world-renowned racing stables such as Vincent O'Brien's at Cashel, Tipperary. Several famous hunts, the Galway Blazers, Bermingham and Scarteen among them, offer facilities to visitors. One-third of Ireland's population goes racing, and an Irish race meeting is a novel experience. There are 140 to choose from, between January and October.

The value of bloodstock sales and jumping contests to Ireland is reflected in the money Ireland spends on its magnificent arenas and computerized sale-ring in Dublin.

It is at an Irish fair, however, that the nation's obsession with horseflesh is most clearly demonstrated. The tinkers (gypsies) are the first to arrive – some in three-litre

Above and below A knowledge of horseflesh and human nature is part of every Irishman's birthright, and the annual horse fair of his local market town (in these pictures Listowel, Kerry) finds him in his element.

Above right Rivalling its English counterpart for colour and prestige, Derby Day at the Curragh of Kildare is red-ringed on the calendars of all who love a contest and a spectacle.

Below right Ireland has been said by an unprejudiced observer (Sir Arnold Bax) to have more melodies and varied folk music than any other land. At the traditional fairs and festivals the Wren Boys, Straw Boys and Biddy Boys are the chief exponents of it.

automobiles with sophisticated mobile homes swinging behind. Horse-dealing is a profitable business for the 'travelling folk'.

Fairground vehicles move in, the sideshows go up, the fair spreads from main street to surrounding meadows. Land Rovers crawl in ever-widening circles, looking for somewhere to park. There are roundabouts, food stalls, fortune-tellers, farm machinery salesmen, card-sharpers, brass bands and ballad singers. Day and night the Wren Boys, Straw Boys and Biddy Boys fiddle away in a frenzy of folksong. A commotion arises in the street: it is only a horse broken loose, and the tinkers' untethered ponies taking fright and the tinkers running about, rounding them up.

Horsy foreigners come to the big traditional fairs – Ballinasloe and Clifden (Galway), Killorglin (Kerry), Tallow (Waterford), Drimoleague (Cork) and others – as eagerly as they do to the Dublin sales, the show-jumping spectaculars and the Leopardstown races. Napoleon more than once sent a commission to purchase cavalry horses in Ireland. A Russian delegate at the Congress of Vienna (1815) thought Ballinasloe was the capital city. But the dedicated buyers and sellers are the Irish farmers.

They dress formally for the fair in dark suits, tweed caps and ties, each carrying a hazel switch. Native optimism and love of horseflesh persuade them that the yearling they will buy is a future Grand National winner. Ireland's lush climate and mild winters make horse-owning cheap for the farmer. He can school the animal himself. In the county hunt, he has on his doorstep the finest of training grounds for a jumper.

A circle of spectators, swaying and shoving, indicate the start of a deal. In the middle is Pat, a possible customer, casually measuring himself against a horse. The owner, Mike, pays no attention to this, nor to Pat's next move, which is to lift the horse's hoof. Buyer and seller engage in non-committal conversation about life in general. 'Will ye trot him?' says Pat at last. Now the business can begin, the crowd presses closer and from it emerges a self-appointed negotiator, probably unknown to Pat or Mike. He is the man who makes the fair go round.

His job is to narrow the gap between asking price and offer. Tireless, good-humoured, voluble, he frequently grabs Mike's hand and slaps it down on Pat's. But he is premature. Each time, one or the other lets his hand drop to his side. After an hour, Pat may simply walk away. Or the negotiator may make the hands stick and that clinches the deal. The crowd's lips move with Pat's as he counts off a roll of dirty banknotes. He makes a chalk-mark on the horse's flank: he will pick it up later. An old-fashioned owner will lay a handful of dirt on the horse's back, to show he is no longer for sale. Buyer and seller equally satisfied, move off.

Thus, to natives and foreign buyers, the world's most prized horses are disposed of. Towards dusk, many visitors are propping cheque-books against horses' rumps or on the bonnets of automobiles, signing with fountain-pens. And many Mikes are stuffing their wallets with banknotes.

After two days or three days, or maybe ten days, the fair begins to break up. Nights are noisy with celebration and the dismantling of timber and canvas. The roads out of town are crowded with processions of trucks, horse-boxes and strings of ponies.

Last of all comes a tinker of the old breed, driving his donkey-cart from the standing position. Four grubby little flaxen-haired girls dangle their legs over the tailboard. This tinker had no horse to sell or buy, but he too was an integral part of the scene. He is trotting west. Down here the fair is over, but out there another fair is about to begin.

Connaught

1 Leitrim 2 Sligo
3 Roscommon 4 Mayo
5 Galway

The western parts of Counties Galway and Mayo have such a reputation for being a neglected wonderland that it is strange they are not congested with solitude-seekers. But this region, 225km (140 miles) from Dublin and 290km (180 miles) from Belfast, is still the lonely corner of Ireland, which itself is the most thinly-populated country in Europe.

It is a windswept corner too. In westerly weather, when the updraught under Connemara's cliffs blows curtains of rain back inland, the orphaned donkeys stand resignedly with heads bowed to the gale and the roads, forging through the stonewalled landscape, are ribbons of running water.

Here on the edge of the Old World, weather systems chase each other rapidly towards the land. Connemara is a rainbow region, a country of flashing moods. People may say here, as they do in Iceland: 'If you don't like our weather, just wait half an hour'. Soon the moors are bathed in sunshine. The wind drops as though turned off at a hydrant. Steam drifts up from the puddles and the traveller discovers that those trees whose fronds were blown out stiff beyond recognition are actually palmettoes.

It is a brilliant country too, more colourful than one expects Ireland's wild west to be. Gorse lies in golden sheets across the well-washed pastures. The pink and purple haze of fuchsia and rhododendron light up mile after mile of hedgerow. On a calm day the Peacock and Red Admiral butterflies come out in clouds. Drystone walls pursue their interminable, monochromatic, wavering line, but a score of tiny quarries flash the wave-green signal of Connemara marble. These quarries employ

Previous page Gleniff, County Sligo, is one of many valleys which carry the peaty, fast-flowing torrents of Connaught to the sea.
Below A traditional cottage at Lettermore conveys the tranquillity of moorland and lough (and the occasional botanical surprise) on the shores of Galway Bay.
Right In such a farmhouse of County Mayo, the playwright J M Synge listened to the chatter of servant girls and learned the dialogue of realism. Transferred to the stage, the rippling vernacular of Mayo shocked Dublin audiences.

only two or three men apiece. Their product is the raw material for Connaught's fireplaces, monuments and craft souvenirs.

Solitude is the grand feature. Beside unfished loughs and salmon rivers, the routes push into empty country. Now and again they drop down to island-studded havens where abandoned customs houses and cattle-pens rot away on derelict jetties. From those rough-and-ready emigration ports of the last century the eye traces the sailing-ship track, out beyond an obstacle course of scattered rocks and into the Atlantic. Probably never again on their two-month voyage were the emigrants so close to disaster as in the first two hours, working clear of Clifden or Westport, Newport or Leenane. When God made the world, they say, he had a

lot of useless stones left over, and he dropped them all in Clew Bay.

In a meadow beside the immaculate little town of Clifden, County Galway, on the edge of the most famous of all Irish bays, a cairn marks the spot where Alcock and Brown crash-landed their aircraft after the first aerial crossing of the Atlantic in 1919. On that spot it seems less of an achievement: the New World appears to be almost nearer than the Old. An elaborate John F Kennedy memorial in Galway Cathedral and a John F Kennedy monument in the main square which takes precedence over Irish heroes, reinforce that impression.

Dropping down on Galway from the hills, one blinks at the sight of double-decker buses with 'City Centre' on their destination boards.

But Galway is a big town by west of Ireland standards: with 36,000 inhabitants, a castle, cathedral, central park, luxury hotel, civic sword and mace, not to mention wynds and crumbling alleyways, the curving tracery of Mediterranean ironwork and a city-within-a-city at the Claddagh. The Claddagh's waterfront of thatched and white-washed cabins where the Corrib river enters Galway Bay has gone, along with its tough, introverted fisher folk. The name today (it simply means 'beach') is chiefly associated with the Claddagh Ring of joined hands clasping a heart – a motif used when Claddagh folk elected their own 'king' and 'council of state'. Tourism has adapted the design for souvenir rings, brooches and tiepins.

Latin ceremonial flavours Galwegian folk-lore, the Blessing of the Sea in mid-August and the Oyster Festival in September. A Galway fisherman sailed with Columbus. The very name Galway means 'a foreign place'. Palmtrees bend over Spanish Arch, iron latticework fringes Spanish Parade, a restaurant has *tortillas espagnolas* on its menu. There are Spanish touches in the granite and Connemara marble of the splendid modern cathedral. The dark eyes of local senoritas (one dare hardly call them colleens) convey a hint of the old trading alliance with Spain. But an early visitor also spoke of this town as a 'wild, fierce and most original' place, and one can still see what he meant.

Tourist shops sell thick off-white, patchwork sweaters in distinctive patterns like trellis, moss and blackberry. These are the 'family'

Below inset Portumna 'Castle' – originally a charming Jacobean mansion, now gutted and empty – stands in a small town well known to waterborne holidaymakers: Portumna guards the Shannon entrance from Lough Derg. The 'Castle' was formerly the seat of Lord Clanricarde, the moneylending marquess and the 19th century's leading miser.

patterns of stitch by which, as readers of JM Synge may recall, mothers of fishermen identified their drowned sons. The sweaters, flannel waistcoats and pampooties (rawhide shoes for rock-scrambling) are the archetypal garments of Aran men. Ireland's favourite offshore rocks, the Aran islands, form a barrier across the approaches to Galway Bay. Until 50 years ago these isles, criss-crossed with claustrophobic stonewalled lanes and dotted with prehistoric drystone forts of which the 27-hectare (11-acre) Dun Aengus was the most spectacular, held remote and primitive communities.

Rough seas made the group almost inaccessible. (They were better connected with America than Connaught. Up to a few years ago, the liner *Statendam* called there en route from New York to Amsterdam.) The islanders had no post, no newspapers, no policeman – 'and no Guinness', says a Galway man. But now there are boats from the Clare and Galway coasts and an air service from Oranmore near Galway city to each of the three islands. They have entered the world and become a tourist attraction.

The mainland north of Galway Bay was the haunt of wild men and potheen makers (illicit whiskey). There are seaside resorts now, but the desolate coasts are no Costa Brava, no pleasure-land for playboys of the western world. They were the homes of Judge Lynch and Captain Boycott, two anti-heroes who put new verbs into the English language (though hereabouts it is Irish which is spoken). 'Joyce's Country' (the name appears thus on the map) covers the most barren hills of Connemara. It is where Joyce the robber baron lorded it over the Fourteen Tribes (reputedly of Welsh origin). Galway bears the legend 'Citie of the Tribes' on its crest. A title some prefer is 'City of Tumbling Waters'.

Landscape and the temperamental humour of countryfolk have fascinated poets and playwrights. W B Yeats's Innisfree, the Lake Isle of his best-known poem, is one of numerous islands in Lough Gill, close to Sligo town, and Dooney Rock, prominent on the wooded shore, inspired his *Fiddler of Dooney*. J M Synge

Above Primeval ice-rivers carried masses of volcanic rock from the mountains down to the Carrowmore district on the outskirts of Sligo town. Prehistoric man adapted the boulder-strewn landscape to his own needs; his cairns and tombs make a strange countryside look stranger. Near Carrowmore there used to be 85 chamber-tombs and passage-graves (dating from about 2500 BC), but their importance was not recognized and only about 20 have been saved from the unconscious vandalism of local landowners. But some villagers are afraid to go near them.
Right South of Sligo Bay the Ox Mountains rise to 550 m (1800 ft). Among them is Ireland's youngest lake: Lough Achree, the result of an earthquake in 1490. Other disturbances turned the hill torrents and an erupting volcano scattered smooth round boulders over the surrounding district.

drew tirelessly on the Galway, Mayo and Sligo character for plots and dialogue in his comedies and tragedies of the struggle for existence against Nature's hostility.

Many Irish myths and fairy stories have their roots in Connaught's far west, and a romping vernacular enriches the tale. County Mayo people do not discount the possibility that an innocent-looking thorn bush may house a Little Family. Connemara villagers have been known to dress their small boys as girls, to deceive the fairies. Archaeologists may call the stone circles of County Sligo 'pre-historic forts', but to local folk they are 'royalties', where the Little People hold their conclaves and society weddings. Villagers carefully examining hedgerows have been rewarded with a sight of the *leprechaun* (fairy shoemaker). Others have heard him at a distance, hammering his nails. In Roscommon and Galway he wears the conventional pointed red cap and red or green coat with fourteen buttons. In County Sligo he is wrapped in a grey topcoat and hugs his crock of gold.

The *dullahan*, the diminutive headless coachman, was spotted in a Sligo street some years ago. Visitors who happen to hear the rumble of tiny ironshod wheels and the clatter of tiny hoofs should beware. To look on the *dullahan* is to be drenched with a bucket of blood.

Intense piety goes with superstitions and primitive beliefs. Croagh Patrick, south of Clew Bay, is the mountain from which Saint Patrick banished all the snakes and vermin from Ireland and it is a fact that these creatures are phenomenally rare.

A papal visit of 1979 informed the world about Knock, a village near Castlebar in County Mayo. That year saw the centenary of a summer evening when about twenty villagers saw representations of the Virgin, St Joseph and St John the Evangelist miraculously projected on a gable wall of the parish church. Lengthy canonical investigations finally pronounced the vision 'trustworthy and satisfactory'. Knock became a holy place, an Irish Lourdes, and now it lies in the shadow of an enormous basilica and of shrines, chapels, tombs of the visionaries and a hospital for sick pilgrims.

When immersed in the rough magic of Connaught's west, it is a shock to come across towns like Westport, County Mayo, much of which remains at its Age of Elegance best. Malls and octagons, bordered by lime trees and a canal-like river, resemble engravings from works on early Georgian town-planning. The British garrisons in the west of Ireland were not popular, but they left behind some graceful and enduring architecture.

Castlebar, county town of Mayo, another military outpost, also has its tree-lined Mall and Regency barracks. The latter are a reminder of a great day for patriots, when a mob with pikes and staves chased the soldiers so fast and so far that the incident passed into history as the 'Castlebar Races'.

Lakes and uplands exposed to sea breezes bring Castlebar into the forefront of touring centres, especially for anglers and walkers. The largest pike known in Britain or Ireland (24 kilos, 53lbs) was taken on Lough Conn, 16km (10 miles) north of Castlebar. The trout, salmon and perch of Loughs Mask, Carra, Cullin and Beltra are also of impressive weight. Shark-fishing is the sport on Achill, Ireland's largest off-shore island. Achill boasts an amethyst quarry, but over most of the island Nature reigns undisturbed, heather blows above sands which know no footprints and the ocean sledge-hammers the cliffs into abstract sculptures.

On the roads of that western lakeland the walker is never out of sight of the combination of golden gorse, moss-green turf and a scintillating sea. Castlebar has capitalized on its situation with a Four-Day Walking Festival. Local walkers lead, follow and mingle with the visitors, spinning yarns as only Connaught people can. Adults, who come from far afield (in 1979 a portly Tasmanian gained only *second* prize for 'farthest to the Festival') are expected to do their 40km (25 miles) per day. The

Enniscrone, or Inishcrone, lies on the east side of Killala Bay, not far from the Ox Mountains. This corner of County Sligo is a desolate land, but only superficially: numerous stone columns and tumuli record the existence of an ancient population. At Lackan (Lecan) Castle close to Enniscrone three priceless chronicles of the Irish, known as the *Books of Lecan*, were written between 1391 and 1671. (They are now in Dublin libraries.)

'miniwalk' for children, minimum age seven, is 14½km (9 miles). It sounds a lot, but something in the air makes the miles flit past and nearly everyone earns a medal. In twelve years of Four-Day Festivals, the only casualty has been a German who sprained an ankle jumping down from a wall. This event is an excuse for much evening merriment and it ends (on the last Sunday in June) with a grand street parade and church service in Castlebar. It is typical of the many off-beat festivals dreamed up by inventive Connaught communities to enliven the summer season. Castlebar is possibly even more celebrated for its annual Song Contest, where substantial rewards are offered to composers and singers of new popular songs (second week in October). Other local festivals which have established themselves in the Irish calendar are the Nephin Festival, named after the highest mountain of the district, at Crossmolina (mid-May); the Ballina Bridge congress (mid-July); the Ballygar show (end of July); and the Currane Games and Regatta on Achill Sound (early August).

Around Ballina and Crossmolina it is water, water everywhere. Whichever route one takes, westward on the romantic Blacksod road or north-east into Counties Sligo and Leitrim, the moorland grows more mountainous, the lakes become more riverine and tortuous and the population centres are smaller and more infrequent. Sligo town (17,000 inhabitants) is the second city of Connaught but it has what in the industrial countries of the world would be regarded as an entirely rural outlook. Sligo and Leitrim, both placed on the outfalls of the loughs and salmon rivers, have known the history of defensive systems which Gaels, Normans and British – invaders, usurpers and landed barons – exploited in their turn. The story of those two counties must have been more dramatic in pre-recorded history, judging by the chamber tombs and standing stones which decorate the hilltops. The region must once have been one of the most densely inhabited in Ireland. Today it is among the quietest places under the sun.

The actual settlement called Leitrim consists

of a few houses only, not marked on ordinary touring maps. It seems to have been chosen to give its name to the county merely to avoid a squabble between the only two towns, Manorhamilton and Carrick-on-Shannon – or perhaps because they were too much of a mouthful. The county town, however, is Carrick-on-Shannon, which dreamed the centuries away until motor-boating holidays became popular. Carrick today is the place where multitudes of visitors begin their Shannon cruises. Flotillas of small craft jam the waterway as the season approaches its climax with the Regatta Carnival (first week in August) and the Boat Rally and Festival (first week in October). County Leitrim is neatly bisected by the infant Shannon and by the first of its lakes, Lough Allen, but the river's source is just over the border, in County Cavan (Ulster).

Of the three major towns of county Roscommon – Roscommon, Castlerea and Boyle – silent streets of low-built stone houses or a drowsy station-house of glittering granite are as much as most passing travellers see. Boyle has

W B Yeats associations, Castlerea was the home of Oscar Wilde's forebears and Roscommon takes its name from Saint Comman, who had a cell on the spot. No trace remains of the abbey he built 1400 years ago, though ecclesiastical records speak highly of it. Of several other, slightly more recent, religious houses and monuments there is hardly enough left visible to stir the imagination.

The scenic side of this agricultural inland county is the lake-shore of Lough Ree, through which the Shannon flows, the great divide between the provinces of Connaught and Leinster. To most foreign visitors, the province of Connaught means Galway and Mayo and Sligo, the shining hills of Connemara, the rock-bespattered inlets and the land of innumerable lakes. To the inhabitants of the greater part of the province, however, it means a spirit of true rusticity, a preoccupation with grazing land and fodder, cattle and donkeys and ponies, a life close to earth and water, a life-style which the Connaught peasant-farmers of 200 years ago would recognize as something like their own.

Craft and Cottage Industry

By the end of the 18th century the population of Ireland was estimated at 16,000,000, half that of England and Scotland combined. For the necessities of life everyone depended on articles made by hand from elemental materials – wool and wood, grasses and stone. Craftsmen and craftswomen pursued ancestral trades and techniques. Monks and nuns perpetuated the traditions of their forebears and the antiquities of the race, with the inspiration of golden-age arts (Book of Kells, Tara brooch, Ardagh chalice, Celtic High Crosses and similar rarities) before them.

Long ago in Ireland, useful meant beautiful. Some practitioners of crafts have maintained the connection down the ages. Although native spinners and boatmakers, blacksmiths and basket-weavers are fewer, the traditional occupations do survive and, under the impact of tourism, are flourishing again. Tourism, while it vulgarizes arts and crafts, does help to preserve them. Some which were hardly known in Ireland in bygone days – pottery, for example – are gaining acceptance.

Both North and South are famous for tweeds, linen and lace. The sheep-rearing districts, notably Donegal, Mayo and Kerry, used to support cottage industries where home-

Above The florid lustreware of Belleek, the most celebrated name in Irish pottery, had its beginnings long ago when clay deposits were found at nearby Castle Caldwell, County Donegal. There are also ancient pottery traditions at Youghal (County Cork), Carley's Bridge (County Wexford) and Coalisland (County Tyrone).
Below Weaving, pottery and ironwork flourish in workshops round the cobbled courtyard of Muckross Abbey.

Right The glass-blowers of Waterford established themselves when 19th-century Irish households began demanding a relatively cheap substitute for silver plate and cutlery. Waterford glass is recognizable by its colourless clarity perfectly free from the bluish tinge. The factory (at Kilbarry, Waterford town) is open to visitors during normal working hours – as are the crystal factories at Galway City, Cavan and Bennettsbridge.

spinners and hand-weavers produced heavy woollens. Now the mills and tweed shops deal in a great variety of garments, from svelte evening gowns to rough shooting jackets. Much cloth is still woven by 'out-workers' in their homes, especially in Donegal. A new kind of hand-weaver has arisen: one who supplies fabrics in light weights and delicate colours, not only for clothing but also for bedspreads, rugs and wall-hangings. Hand-knitted handbags, lace dresses and even crocheted Bermuda shorts, done to the designs of top *couturiers*, are among the new lines in textiles.

Some Irish linen, too, is made, bleached and dyed by individual workers, although there are factories turning out synthetic materials with the so-called 'linen look'. Linen and crochetwork are specialities of the northern counties and Carrickmacross lace still comes from the convent in County Monaghan which started making it two centuries ago.

Cut crystal is an old craft which almost died out, but during the past thirty years it has begun to flourish as never before. Galway, Dublin and various centres in County Cavan have their glass industries and in recent years Northern Ireland has come to the forefront with its Tyrone crystal. The purest and most elaborate cut crystal is found in the most venerable centre of the craft, Waterford.

Pottery studios recently established in West Cork and Counties Dublin, Kilkenny and Clare are injecting typically Irish fantasy and individuality into ceramics. A metropolis of pottery is Belleek, County Fermanagh, a village with (unusually for Ireland) clay deposits on which the foundations of a famous lustreware were laid. A potter in Carley's Bridge, Wexford, sells ware on premises which have housed his ancestors' wheel and kiln for 400 years.

One does not immediately associate Ireland with precious stones or minerals, but there are marcasite and dolomite in County Kilkenny, diatomite in Antrim, copper in Limerick, Tipperary and Cork, silver in County Galway and amethyst on Achill island, Mayo. The ubiquitous green Connemara marble is mined in Galway's far west. Silver, gold and enamel workers are found all over the country, as are artists in Celtic jewelry who keep the native stone and metal crafts alive. In Dublin, Belfast, Derry, Cork and the towns of County Tipperary some fascinating jewelry is on sale. There are rings, brooches and ornaments of archaic design and vaguely ecclesiastical character, interpreted in the modern manner, and river pebbles and semi-precious stones set in intricately-worked beaten silver. Certain antique shops specialize in old Irish silver, in 'potato rings' and other inimitable examples of the silversmith's skill.

Around horse-breeding centres – the Curragh of County Kildare particularly – decorative leather and ironwork are produced by the descendants of the old-time saddlers and farriers. In country districts of the midlands and west, where slow-paced rivers and cornfields too tiny for mechanical harvesting allow the raw material to thrive, the woven baskets and rush mats once found in every Irish rustic homestead are still made and sold, along with basketry utensils and ornaments. The woven cross of Saint Brigid (Ireland's patroness and the saint of spinners and weavers) is a popular line among the many visitors to this area.

For a costly souvenir, a visitor might look in at a famous Dublin music shop for a made-to-order Irish harp or other traditional instrument. For a cheap memento the crooked blackthorn stick (*shillelagh*), the briar pipe and the bog-oak carving are always available. The tourist authorities of both Northern Ireland and the Republic exercise strict control on souvenir items. By following their guidance, whether at Shannon Airport's gigantic shopping precinct or a humble village store in remote Donegal, the purchaser can usually be confident of paying a fair price for a guaranteed craft object.

Ulster

1 Donegal 2 Cavan
3 Monaghan 4 Fermanagh
5 Tyrone 6 Londonderry
7 Antrim 8 Down 9 Armagh

Previous page The quiet
metropolis of Rathlin Island off the
Antrim coast, scene of Bruce's
adventure with the spider.
Below Belfast, growing fast from
almost nothing in late Victorian
times, is not notable for its
architecture. Belfast Castle is
among the more impressive
buildings. Built for the Marquess
of Donegall in 1867, it 'went
public' in 1934 and its large park is
one of the favourite recreation
areas of the citizens.
Right With elaborate wood-
carving and floor-tiling, the old-
time publican of Belfast gave his
establishment an exclusive air.
This is the Crown Bar in Great
Victoria Street.

Ulster was the Anglo-Norman earldom, seized and held in the 14th century by the O'Neills, rampaging Irish warlords. During the 17th century the Stuart kings and the protector Oliver Cromwell recovered it for Britain. Thereafter it was settled by Scottish and English Protestants in the notorious 'Plantations' and parcelled out into nine counties. When Ireland broke with Britain in 1921, six north-eastern counties which had historical and geographical links with Britain remained British. The other three were incorporated in the Irish Free State, which in 1948 became the Republic of Ireland.

Ulster's partition has brought about a confusion of nomenclature which non-residents have to stop and think about. It is a province divided between two nations, and the word Ulster no longer has administrative meaning. Southern Irishmen call Northern Ireland the 'Six Counties', or simply 'the North'. Northern Irishmen call the Republic the 'Twenty-six Counties', or 'the South'. (The Gaelic word *Eire*, the old name for Ireland, is printed on the Republic's postage-stamps but is not much used among English speakers. Strictly speaking, the word refers to the whole island.)

Two typical anomalies of the position are that Ireland's most northerly point, Malin Head, is actually in the South; and that Belfast, historically the most wildly republican of cities, is currently the most stridently attached to the British crown.

The North is different from the South; especially around Belfast. Towns and villages are more formal in style, the municipal organizations are tidier, roads and 'road furniture' are built to costlier standards. Industrialization has made them so. Even a century ago, three-quarters of Ireland's industrial wealth was concentrated in the Belfast area. The biggest reservoir of labour is still there. The rest of Ireland, compared to Counties Down and Antrim, appears to be an under-developed land, in quiet harmony with nature.

Northern Ireland's capital city, Belfast, has long been a hotbed of bankers, merchants and shopkeepers. Linen, washed and bleached in the Lagan valley above Belfast Lough, was the foundation of Northern Ireland's prosperity at a time when no one calling himself a gentleman wore shirts of anything but linen, and every lady carried a linen handkerchief. When cotton replaced linen, hard-headed Belfast manufacturers were ready for the change.

The mills employed chiefly women and girls. It was yet another far-sighted industrialist, EJ Harland, who provided jobs for the men. He was the first shipbuilder to appreciate that the new iron vessels required different constructional techniques from the old wooden ones. The firm of Harland & Wolff was born. A sea-channel was dug in the Lagan river to bring big ships into the heart of the city. By 1914, Belfast formed a corner of a powerful 'economic triangle' with Glasgow in Scotland (225km, 140 miles away) and Liverpool in England (256km, 160 miles away).

'We find in Ulster,' wrote J W Woodburn (*The Ulster Scot*, 1915) 'the largest linen manufactory, the largest shipbuilding yard, the largest rope-making factory, the largest tobacco factory and the largest mineral water factory in the world. The success of the people of Belfast ... is a striking proof of what energy and perseverance will accomplish. The city of Belfast ... has to import every pound of iron and every ton of coal, and yet the spirit and enterprise of the Ulsterman have enabled him to surmount these obstacles.'

Perhaps it goes without saying then that Belfast lacks the dreamy charm of other Irish towns and cities, that a down-to-earth seriousness is in the air and that many citizens have lived with inadequate housing since the beginning of the century (when the population doubled itself in 25 years). Belfast has known hard times, but in recession has had the economic strength of Great Britain to fall back on. The Second World War renewed its prosperity. New technology has created jobs in the scientific and light and heavy engineering industries and in the shipyards. Despite inducements to foreign firms to set up in business in other areas of Northern Ireland, Belfast and its environs still exercise the greatest influence on them.

The public buildings and institutions are, for a capital city, somewhat undistinguished. Belfast Castle is much visited, not for its history (it was built in 1867) but for the city park, pleasure gardens, zoo and hill of caves which surround it. The outstanding Belfast buildings are Stormont Castle and Parliament houses, a triumphant essay in the 1930s 'government classical' style;

and the Grand Opera House, brilliantly refurbished in 1980.

On the south side of Belfast is the large and expanding Queen's University, nowadays almost a university city, with botanical gardens adjoining. (Another Irish anomaly is that the principal seat of learning in the Protestant North is a Catholic foundation, whereas the principal one in the Catholic South – Trinity College, Dublin – is a Protestant one.) Once a year the students of Queen's and Trinity meet on opposite banks of the Boyne river for a tug-of-war. The rope is stretched across the water, so the losers cannot help falling in.

The second city of Northern Ireland, and the second largest in the province of Ulster, is Derry – more properly called Londonderry, a name it received when King James I of England in 1613 granted the town and its countryside to the citizens of London. Derry today is fundamentally the planned city enclosed in massive walls (the most complete set of walls in the British Isles) which expatriate Londoners built

in the 17th century. The most memorable event of Derry's history occurred towards the end of the same century, when townsfolk successfully withstood a six-months' siege by Jacobite forces attempting a Stuart restoration.

Within recent memory, Derry's strategic position at the head of the long, deep and sheltered Lough Foyle has made it an important base for the British Navy and Air Force. The town still has its seaborne trade. Some of Northern Ireland's textile and clothing industries, including a major concentration of shirt and pyjama manufacturers, are centred on Derry, but unemployment is now high.

On the shores and waters of Lough Foyle, the visitor finds a scenic holiday spot which seems remote from any industrial town. On the Donegal side the hills of Inishowen slope gently to the neat resort of Moville, ancestral home of Field-Marshal Montgomery. Near Glenagivny, local sub-aqua divers have raised from the wreck of a Spanish galleon of 1588 the finest known collection of cannon of that era. The calm waters of Lough Foyle funnel down to a seaward entrance through which boats must proceed in single file. On the County Derry shore, the silver strand of Magilligan, 9½km (6 miles) long, stretches to the mouth of Limavady's river. It was near Limavady, 'on the road to Derry town one day', that the composer of the world's best-loved song picked up the melody of *The Londonderry Air* from a wandering musician.

A tour along the coast roads is probably the best introduction to Ulster. And Donegal Bay, the broadest and most majestic in Ireland, is probably the best starting-point. Donegal, a land of primitive dwellings, tiny communities, stone-age relics, wild seascapes and coloured cliffs backing on to craggy granite mountains, is a fashionable county for quiet holiday living. Villages dot the havens all round Donegal's western and northern inlets. The play of light and shadow on the naked rock produces kaleidoscopic effects (Bloody Foreland is so-named for that headland's appearance in a stormy sunset). Little places like Enniscrone and Bundoran, Carrigart and Rosapenna, live partly on tourism and partly by craftwork of an unpretentious kind. (But the tweeds of Gweedore and the hand-tufted carpets of Killybegs are famous far beyond Ireland's coastline.)

From the other two counties of the Republic, Monaghan and Cavan, an extraordinary system of lakes and islands makes an almost continuous water-corridor from the eastern districts of Ulster to the Donegal coast at Ballyshannon. Romantically sited on an island at the neck of water linking Upper and Lower Lough Erne is the town and star-shaped fort of Enniskillen, County Fermanagh. It was the key to the military dispositions of the region and its history through the turbulent 17th century was of continual capture and recapture by the Irish Maguires and the English troops. Descendants of the warring factions eventually combined to form two renowned British regiments, the Inniskilling Dragoon Guards and the Royal Inniskilling Fusiliers.

Among the countless lakes (County Monaghan has nearly 200 and Fermanagh across the Northern Ireland border might well be called the county of 1000 islands) are circular tower forts and Georgian mansions which hint at man's centuries-long preoccupation with pike and perch, bream and rudd and other coarse fish. Angling hereabouts is a way of life; yet the fish breed ever more prolifically under banks of disintegrated limestone in the maze of slow-flowing rivers and stagnant backwaters.

At the Donegal end of the lower lough, Belleek is noted for an old-established porcelain production. At the Enniskillen end there stands a sculpted Round Tower 25m (81ft) high, acknowledged to be the handsomest in Ireland, and alongside it is an ecclesiastical showplace, Devenish Abbey. Even these reminders of a cultivated past seem commonplace against the mysterious and grotesque carved stones on White Island in the lough. They are reminiscent of the figures on Easter Island and are known to date from the 9th century AD.

Monks once inhabited Pettigoe, a market village which belongs both to Northern Ireland and the Republic as the county boundary between Fermanagh and Donegal follows the village stream down the main street. Here on a barren rock in Lough Derg pilgrims to a cave associated with Saint Patrick's 'purgatory' submit to severe disciplines: bare feet, all-night vigils, no heating, one daily meal of dry bread and 'Lough Derg soup' (water). The pilgrim season is from early June to mid-August and only those who accept the routine are allowed to land on the island.

Eastward through Ulster the routes thread through the pastoral landscape of Counties Tyrone and Armagh. Hills are smooth and round and the dairy farms – though relatively small – are responsible for a high proportion of the United Kingdom's butter, milk and egg production. Journey's end is a sophisticated coastline of golf-course and bathing beach.

Portrush, County Antrim, is the biggest Ulster resort and has the grandest situation. Its

Above Burtonport faces a maze of islets south of Bloody Foreland. Deep channels, sheltered waters and rich off-shore fisheries on this desolate Donegal coast prompted philanthropic noblemen to invest in harbour schemes. Rutland Island commemorates an abortive development of 1785 by the English Duke of Rutland. The Irish Marquess Conyngham had better luck at nearby Burtonport on the mainland. It became a busy herring port and even acquired a picturesque meandering rail link with Letterkenny and Derry City.

hinterland is the Irish whiskey country of Bushmills and Coleraine. A neighbouring promontory consists of the geological phenomenon known as the Giant's Causeway. The mass of polygonal basalt columns (open to the public since 1963) suggested to the Celtic imagination a series of stepping-stones to Scotland, which at this point is only 48km (30 miles) away. One

man alone could have built it or used it: Finn MacCool, the Fingal of Pictish mythology. The same ogre is credited with having scooped up a handful of Ulster earth and thrown it into the sea. The earth became the Isle of Man and the hole it left became Lough Neagh. The latter, the largest lake in the British Isles 392sq km (153sq miles) is also the most featureless, being noted

for eels and pollan trout and very little else.

The north-eastern coast is not spectacular but the configuration of sea-lough and isthmus is strange enough to have spawned many a legend. Finn MacCool is only one of a number of wonderful creatures who have had a hand in shaping the topography, according to Down and Antrim folklore.

The fortress at Ballycastle, County Antrim, was built in a single night, they say. The grave of Ossian, son of Finn MacCool, is pointed out a few miles south, in the Glens of Antrim. Northern Ireland's proximity to Scotland, only 24km (15 miles) away at the shortest crossing, has attracted dubious tales from the mainland. Robert the Bruce is known to have sought

All routes from Dublin to Belfast traverse flat country until they reach the inappropriately-named County Down, where the hills begin. This view, from the Slieve Donard Hotel, is an Ulster classic: the resort of Newcastle (whose castle was new four centuries ago), noted for sandy beaches and dunes and the Royal County Down golf course, nestling in a hollow where the Mountains of Mourne sweep down to the sea.

refuge on Rathlin Island, Antrim, while fleeing from the English in 1306. A cave on Rathlin is supposed to have been the scene of Bruce's object-lesson from the spider.

Saint Patrick, we are told, was a shepherd boy on the Slemish mountain, which overlooks the ferry port of Larne. The story goes that he came back to Ulster to die, and that his bones are laid under a church he founded at Downpatrick, County Down. The church has become the Protestant cathedral. The headstone inscribed PATRIC is a Victorian embellishment.

Real history is threaded on to fiction at Carrickfergus, supposedly the site of the death by drowning of Prince Fergus from whom the early kings of Scotland claimed descent. The castle, subject of many paintings and picture-postcards, dates back to the 12th century and is well preserved. Watchers on its towers in 1778 saw the warship *Ranger*, Captain John Paul Jones in command, fight the first action and secure the first victory of American arms in European waters.

South of Belfast Lough the routes head back to the Republic's border and to Dublin. Along the coast, the Ards peninsula, Strangford Lough (almost an inland sea), the South Down shore and Carlingford Lough (before it narrows to a muddy channel at the quays of Newry), are a ribbon of seaside places, golf courses and yachting centres. Bangor, County Down, is now called Belfast-by-the-Sea; before the Vikings ravaged this coast in the 9th century, Bernard of Clairvaux named it Nursery of Saints. Many of Ireland's saints and scholars were trained there at Saint Comgall's abbey, founded in about 555.

Newcastle and Kilkeel are the smart resorts of the southern Down shore. Between them runs Slieve Donard (852m, 2796ft), a viewpoint for six 'kingdoms' – England, Ireland, Scotland, Wales, Mann (Isle of Man) and Heaven. Donard

.or Domangard was another Ulster saint, son of the last pagan king and guardian of the mountain who lived in about 500 AD. The archaeology of the district is littered with Donard's cairns, Donard's caves, Donard's footprints and similar fanciful names.

Only a valley away, and on the southern limits of the province, the Mourne country begins: hilltracks, heathery pastures, up-hill-and-down-dale lanes. A walker has the illusion of striding over continental spaces instead of being cooped up in a little province barely 100km (60 miles) wide.

'Where the Mountains of Mourne sweep down to the sea' is from one of the songs of Percy French, who was born in the marsh country of Cavan. A humble inspector of drains, he had no ambition to be a millionaire songwriter. He sold outright, for modest fees, the copyrights of lyrics which others made fortunes out of: *The Mountains of Mourne, Phil the Fluter's Ball, Come Back Paddy Reilly, The Pride of Petravore* and dozens more. There are people still alive who remember him gathering children round him on the beach at Kilkeel or Newcastle, Skerries or Howth – doing lightning sketches on a blackboard and spinning a tale to go with them, advising on the building of sandcastles, decorating buckets and spades with a matchstick and a smoky candle and fixing the design with white of egg. 'The kind of man,' says an old Newry landlady, 'who'd paint a water-colour and give it away, and soon you'd see it in a gallery priced at 15 pounds.'

Percy French has been criticized for propagating a childish view of Ireland and the Irish, for sentimentalizing things as they never were. He was, of course, a man of his time – the Edwardian era. He had enormous talent, and used it to please and entertain others. He was a typical Ulsterman of the old school, a generous and good-natured person.

Castle, House and Garden

Visitors pursuing hobbies of diverse kinds find in Ireland their particular paradise. But for none is Ireland more a happy hunting ground than for the lover of country houses, the zealot for castles, the indefatigable examiner of stately homes and gardens. Almost every parish has its noble mansion or fortress of gloomy memory. Climate, and the social structure of the past, favoured the landscaping of lakes and gardens. Many of them are tended with care and affection to this day. A sizeable proportion of these properties, frequently with their owners in residence, are accessible to the public. By arrangement with the Historic Irish Tourist Houses Association and the National Trust's Northern Ireland committee, visitors may do a circuit of stately homes with banquets and sherry parties included.

Architectural distinction, rare plants and unspoiled demesnes are not all. Some great houses have programmes of concerts and recitals, others host flower-arranging festivals, poetry readings and dramatic performances, summer schools and exhibitions, archery meetings and steam-engine rallies.

The vast grey country mansions are a credit to old Ireland. They tend to be larger than life, and sometimes a bit wobbly in the upper storey. Their owners seem to have lived by the motto 'Expense no Object'. It takes 90 minutes to walk from the sea-god fountain (affectionately known as the Spittin' Man) at Powerscourt to the showpiece of the park, which is nothing less than the highest waterfall in the British Isles (121m, 398ft). From 180m (200 yards) of wrought ironwork and mosaic-pebbled pavement, tier upon tier of stone steps proceed towards the Sugar Loaf mountain 755m (2475ft), while a good slice of County Wicklow edges into the vista. And one is not yet out of the demesne, one is not even out of the garden and its maze of urns and statuary.

Powerscourt is among the grandest of Irish estates. Another is Castletown, County Kildare (now headquarters of the influential Irish Georgian Society), a place of Palladian grandeur and magnificent stucco work. Carton, in the same county, is built on a lavish scale too, with spacious landscaped park, lodges, bridges, planted trees and a Shell Cottage inlaid with sea-shells, to which Queen Victoria was rowed in a boat. Those three estates, whose bounds are measured in miles rather than yards, are spread near Dublin's doorstep, on land ripe for suburban development. They are powerful symbols of the centuries when Anglo-Norman

and Anglo-Saxon held sway (and now and again an astute
Dublin politician), when Irish labour was plentiful and
servants cost nothing for (as the Duke of Cambridge said
during the Great Famine) everyone knew that the Irish could
live on anything; 'so let them eat grass'.

The castles and stately homes are not, with a few
exceptions, treasuries of arts or museums of aristocratic
refinement. Seigneurial and military Ireland went in more
for hunting and shooting, burning and hanging, than for fine
furniture, tapestries and paintings. The chief attractions for
the visitor are the architectural follies and botanical
eccentricities, the bric-à-brac and the legends. At Howth,
County Dublin, there is the blaze of rhododendrons, visible
far out to sea, raised from peat carried laboriously, a
bucketful at a time, to fill up all the crevices in the cliffs; this is
also the castle with the beech hedge which takes four months

Left, top A view from the terrace at
Powerscourt, County Wicklow, with the
Sugar Loaf mountain in the background.
Left, bottom Castletown, County Kildare,
headquarters of the Irish Georgian Society.

Above left Abbey Leix, County Laois,
adjoining the famous gardens of Mount
Stewart.
Below Temple of the Winds, County
Down, built on a monastic site.

Above Westport House, County Mayo,
has been the seat of the Brownes
(Marquesses of Sligo) since it was built in
1730 – one might say since Tudor times,
for the Brownes claim descent from Grace
O'Malley, ferocious Amazon of Connaught,
who tormented her captives in dungeons
on this very spot. The house was enlarged
at various periods. The entrance hall is
early Georgian, with excellent stucco work
and a fine barrel-vaulted ceiling. The
staircase beyond, made in Sicilian marble,
is high Victorian.

every year to clip; the castle where two places are set daily at
table, by order of Grace O'Malley, Queen of the West 400
years ago, for guests who will never return.

Tullynally, County Westmeath, boasts a private gas-
works and the oldest central heating system in the British
Isles. Abbey Leix, County Laois, has the oldest oak-tree in
Europe and the grave of an Irish king. Birr Castle, County
Offaly, claims the largest telescope in the world – or did,
until Mount Palomar's was built. (Birr is the home of the
Parsons, Earls of Rosse, a scientific family. With his home-
made 'Great Telescope' the third earl discovered the spiral
nature of nebulae in 1847. His elder son was the first
astronomer to take the temperature of the moon, and his
younger, Charles Parsons, invented the steam turbine.)

Clonalis, County Roscommon, keeps the harp of the last
Irish bard, blind Turlough O'Carolan. Thoor Ballylee,
County Galway, gaunt and foursquare, contains relics of
W B Yeats, who lived there for twelve years. Mount Usher,
County Wicklow, displays more than 70 varieties of
eucalyptus tree among its freak Australasian plants and
shrubs, and Rowallane in County Derry arranges its exotica
in a descending series of self-contained gardens wherein the
flora of foreign lands from China to Chile are reproduced.

Mussenden, County Derry, is a 200-year-old classical
temple in romantic surroundings – a palatial little rotunda on
a clifftop. The Temple of the Winds, overlooking Strangford Lough, County Down, is a rotunda of the same date, a
replica of the pagan temple of that name in Athens, cleverly
adapted to a snug house.

The follies and frivolities (and the superlatives) are thickly
strewn over Irish estates, and the tallest tales in the world go
with them. Where properties have been in the same hands for
centuries, the very names of the owners are worth the price
of admission. Who could resist a few hours under the roof of
the Viscount Gort, the Earl of Cork and Orrery, the
O'Conor Don, Viscount de Vesci, the O'Donoghue of the
Glens, the Earl of Dunraven and Mount Earl, the Knight of
Glin, the Marquess of Sligo, the O'Grady of Killyballyowen
or the MacDermot Prince of Coolavin?

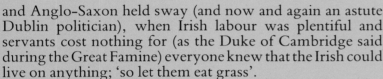

The Shannon

The source of the River Shannon is in Ulster, its route forms the boundary between Connaught and Leinster and its estuary is in Munster. All four provinces, therefore, lend the longest river in the British Isles (338km, 210 miles) their climate, character and scenery.

The Shannon is disproportionately long for such a relatively small country. What is more, it incorporates lakes which give it the largest inland water area in Britain or Ireland. Except where it passes through two modest towns, Athlone and Limerick, nowhere is it urbanized. For almost its entire length it winds through a tranquil countryside and the richness and variety of its wildlife and fisheries proclaim it the least-polluted stream in Europe. Though navigable for 224km (140 miles), it has no industrial traffic. (Holiday craft, however, can cause congestion at the annual boat rallies in Carrick-on-Shannon, Athlone, Shannon Harbour and Lough Derg.)

The gaping ruins of graceful country mansions and the shells of barrack-like Georgian hotels nod over its banks. There was a time when the Shannon was seen as a grand commercial highway, the principal artery of a waterways system which would turn Ireland into a gridiron of canals and deep-water channels. Hence the industrial archaeology of its route, the 19th-century locks (six in all) whose weed-encrusted walls tower over holiday boats. Shannon Harbour, at the midpoint of the river's journey, used to be the cross-roads for passenger barges (with eating and sleeping accommodation 'superior to any inn in Ireland') coming down the Grand Canal from Dublin. Now there remains only a wharf and a disused hotel. But here and there, thanks to tourism, some of the venerable Shannon boatyards and backwaters are in business again.

From the gorse-clad moorland below the Shannon Pot in northern Cavan, the infant river escapes, takes in a couple of small loughs and quickly grows to navigable size. Lough Ree is a stern test for amateur sailors: it is dotted with islets and pitted with unmarked rocks and can be squally and rough.

Below Athlone the river forgets its turbulent youth and becomes the 'lordly Shannon', strolling in a dignified manner through its domains, turning to right and left to cast an eye over its property. County and provincial boundaries conform to its vagaries. Black and red marker buoys and beacons on monolithic cairns dug out of its bed suggest that the river is nearing the sea – but the sea is 193km (120 miles)

Previous page An overnight anchorage for cruising boats is no problem on the calm reaches and among the reed-fringed isles of the Shannon River. (Photograph by Eric Coltham).
Right Below Limerick the Shannon meets the sea. Near its north bank the new town of Shannon has arisen. Its inter-continental airport and duty-free enclave have attracted many foreign industrial companies.
Below At Shannon Harbour, County Offaly, 120 km (75 m) from Dublin, the Grand Canal slips unobtrusively into the great river.

away. Clumps of reeds and tables of rock obstruct the current's slow majestic sweep. No fewer than eight of the biggest islands, streamlined by the flow, are called Long Island.

This is the 'quiet watered land' of the poem *Clonmacnois*, with cornfields, soggy turf, stunted hawthorns, cattle silently standing and a prolific growth of bulrushes. Only the river, winding in S-bends, and the herons, drifting away at the approach of a cabin cruiser, bring the landscape to life. At Clonmacnois itself, boat travellers land and go for a walk among the ruins: Saint Kieran's castle, leaning out at a precarious angle; the Seven Churches and the knolls where the Seven Kings of Tara and the warriors of Erin in their famous generations were laid to rest. 'Many a blue eye of Clan Colman the turf covers,' says the poem, 'many a swan-white breast.'

After Portumna the scenery changes. Meadows and grazing cattle give way to woodland and the rising hills where Silvermines and Dolla recall old-time mineralogical exploits. The rough slopes of Tipperary drop to the edge of Lough Derg, the Shannon's most formidable lake. The chart bristles with hazards like Nut Island, Fathead Rock and The Ninnies – names indicating a certain lack of sympathy with any sailor who comes to grief on them. Guide books tell of fishermen drowned in Lough Derg's notorious squalls and of seagoing vessels capsized while running for shelter in its reef-bespattered inlets.

From the Shannon's middle course, causeway tracks penetrate bog and furze, apparently going nowhere. But they skirt the land of *Bord na Móna* (Irish Peat Board), where 8,000,000 tons of milled peat for Irish power stations, peat 'brickeens' for domestic use and peat moss to enrich market gardens as far afield as the Canary Islands are produced annually by a community of 6000 workers.

This is where the mechanical monsters browse – vehicles of unearthly yet sophisticated design, built on the bog and doomed by their size never to leave it. At slow speed they travel the 18-km (11-mile) 'cutaway' to scour, munch, aerate, press and stockpile the 'black gold'. Miniature trains carry the peat away over the calm brown sea of the bog. Bord na Móna village, church and railway station lie locked away in what was for centuries a swampy, dangerous country, a death-trap for Clonmacnois pilgrims and a region formerly inhabited by bog folk celebrated only for their squalor and ignorance, and by fugitives from justice.

The Peat Board arranges tours for visitors at the Boora, near Kilcormac; also to the peat briquette factory at Derrinlough and the laboratories and museum at Newbridge in County Kildare. In the museum there are flower-pots, cardboard cartons, handkerchiefs, even toothpaste and after-shave lotion, all made from peat, a commodity of which Ireland, however distressful, was never short. An observation car on the little railway provides a figure-of-eight excursion over the vast level plain of the bog. The great experience is to step on to the 'black gold' itself: a trampoline-like turf, with a life of its own. The very monotony of the scene sharpens the senses. From a great way off come the whirr of the bog juggernauts, the clatter of the small train and the shouts of children in a Peat Board village playground. Memorable sunrises and sunsets are created by the dust from this bogland peat. Among those unexpected, unadvertised novelties which crop up in every traveller's path through Ireland, the small world of Bord na Móna is outstanding, yet scarcely known to tourists.

Southward on the Shannon, the lilliputian cottages and pack-donkey bridge of Killaloe announce tourist country once more, a land of easy living and smart riverside hotels and a stream ruffled only by the intersecting furrows of the water-skiers. The last bridge (Sarsfield Bridge) straddles the river at Limerick, third city of Ireland, with 50,000 inhabitants divided between its Irish Town and English Town of military and patriotic history. Here the river begins to surrender to the ocean – but 72km (45 miles) further on from Limerick it is still only 5km (3 miles) wide. The left bank holds a history of eccentric technology: a disappointed transatlantic seaplane base at Foynes, relics of the only monorail track in the British Isles (built 1888, closed 1925) at Listowel. The right bank has two technological success stories: the Shannon hydro-electric scheme at Ardnacrusha and the international airport, Shannon, which has stimulated industrial development.

The river supports Europe's second largest salmon hatchery, operated by the Electricity Supply board. Test drillings for gas and oil on the Continental Shelf indicate an industrial future for the estuary.

Left On the higher reaches of the Shannon holiday cabin cruisers come to their moorings.

Below and right Where the river sweeps out to sea sailing craft drive or drift on the tide.

Index

Page numbers in italics refer to illustrations.

Acknowledgments

The publishers wish to thank the following individuals and organizations for their kind permission to reproduce the photographs in this book:

Bord Fáilte/Irish Tourist Board: 1, 2–3, 6–7, 8–9, 10–11, 12–13, 14–15, 16–17, 18–19, 21 centre, 22–23, 24–25, 26–27, 28–29, 30–31, 32–33, 34–35, 36–37, 38–39, 40–41, 42–43, 44–45, 46–47, 48–49, 50–51, 52–53, 54–55, 56–57, 58–59, 60 below, 61, 66–67, 72, 73 above left, 73 right, 76–77, 78–79; Northern Ireland Tourist Board: 60 above, 62–63, 65, 68–69, 70–71, 73 below; Barnaby's Picture Library: 64; The Mansell Collection 20, 21 above and below left, 21 right; Motor Boat and Yachting, Eric Coltham: 74–75; N. Poulter: endpapers.